The Tomb of Oedipus

William Marx is a French writer and scholar, professor of comparative literatures at the Collège de France, a member of the Academia Europaea, and an honorary fellow of the Institute of Advanced Studies in Berlin. His books, *The Hatred of Literature* among them, have been translated into ten languages.

The Tomb of Oedipus

Why Greek Tragedies Were Not Tragic

William Marx

Translated by Nicholas Elliott

VERSO

London • New York

This English-language edition first published by Verso 2022
Translation © Nicholas Elliott 2022
First published as *Le Tombeau d'Œdipe:
Pour une tragédie sans tragique*
© Editions de Minuit 2012

This book has been published with the support
of the Fondation du Collège de France.

1 3 5 7 9 10 8 6 4 2

Verso
UK: 6 Meard Street, London W1F 0EG
US: 388 Atlantic Avenue, Brooklyn, NY 11217
versobooks.com

Verso is the imprint of New Left Books

ISBN-13: 978-1-78873-613-8
ISBN-13: 978-1-78873-617-6 (UK EBK)
ISBN-13: 978-1-83976-618-3 (US EBK)

British Library Cataloguing in Publication Data
A catalogue record for this book is available from the British Library

Library of Congress Cataloging-in-Publication Data
Names: Marx, William, 1966- author. | Elliott, Nicholas, translator.
Title: The tomb of Oedipus : why Greek
tragedies were not tragic / William
    Marx ; translated by Nicholas Elliott.
Other titles: Tombeau d'Œdipe. English
Description: Brooklyn : Verso, 2022. |
Includes bibliographical references
    and index.
Identifiers: LCCN 2022024390 (print) |
LCCN 2022024391 (ebook) | ISBN
    9781788736138 (trade paperback) | ISBN 9781788736183 (ebook)
Subjects: LCSH: Greek drama (Tragedy)—History and criticism.
Classification: LCC PA3131 .M34313 2022
(print) | LCC PA3131 (ebook) |
    DDC 882/.0109—dc23/eng/20220611
LC record available at https://lccn.loc.gov/2022024390
LC ebook record available at https://lccn.loc.gov/2022024391

Typeset in Sabon by Biblichor Ltd, Scotland
Printed and bound by CPI Group (UK) Ltd, Croydon CR0 4YY

Contents

Introduction

How Does Greek Tragedy Matter to Us?

In one of his most famous stories, Jorge Luis Borges describes the philosopher Averroës's inability to understand the meaning of the two principal words in Aristotle's *Poetics*: *comedy* and *tragedy*. In the Arab civilization of the twelfth century, there is no theatre: Averroës has never seen a play; he knows absolutely nothing about it.

His failure would be cruel enough as it is, but is exacerbated by a particular irony: in the courtyard of the house, children play at imitating adults. The philosopher distracts himself by watching the children, never suspecting that he is looking at the object of his search: the secret of theatre is right before his eyes, and he does not see it.[1]

Faced with Greek tragedy, we are all like Averroës, but unaware of our ignorance. At least the Arab philosopher knew that he did not know. For our part, we think we know tragedy: we have read and studied it at school, seen it on stage, and made the pilgrimage to Athens and Epidaurus. Aeschylus, Sophocles and Euripides are more than names to

---

1 Jorge Luis Borges, 'Averroës' Search' [1947], in *The Aleph: Collected Fictions*, trans. Andrew Hurley (New York: Viking Penguin, 1998), 235–41. Borges explicitly took the subject of this short story from the historical essay *Averroès et l'averroïsme* (Paris: Durand, 1852), 36; here, Ernest Renan explains that having imagined that 'tragedy was nothing but the art of praising, and comedy the art of criticizing', Averroës thought he 'found tragedies and comedies . . . even in the Koran'.

us: we know their work, we have enjoyed it and sometimes even found it admirable.

So? What's the problem?

The fact is that none of all this really makes up Greek tragedy – or Attic tragedy, to be more precise. At best, what we know are its vestiges. Astounding vestiges, surely, which as a whole form one of the greatest achievements of the human spirit. But vestiges nonetheless.

Twenty-four centuries have passed, and all that is left are ruins. Ruins so beautiful that we think we're dealing with the actual works, as if the Venus de Milo were not missing two arms. A terrible illusion.

What happened between Greek tragedy and us? Everything. Obviously, language, religion, and culture are no longer the same. The texts, documents and monuments have nearly all been lost. Only a few scraps have survived this total catastrophe.

But that's not all: between tragedy and us, *literature* came along. For a little more than two centuries, we have been living with an art of language which we have an unwitting tendency to apply to everything that existed before. We read ancient texts through the insidious filter of an autonomous art, intended to be universal, of a superior intellectual level, and detached as much as possible from its context – the places, periods, and gods. Yet no such *literature* existed in the Athens of the fifth century BCE.

So what was there? To try to find out is to go in search of aliens: should Martians one day arrive to perform their plays before our amazed eyes, they would not appear more exotic to us than the masterpieces of Aeschylus and Sophocles would, if we were only willing to see them for what they are – or if we could rediscover them as they were.

The solution is to get rid of received ideas. To launch into a process of defamiliarization. To learn what tragedy is not.

To approach it in a vacuum. To explain it – this only seems like a paradox – by its mystery.

When a crime has been committed, the leading suspect is the last witness to have seen the victim. We will proceed in the same manner. We will start from the last known tragedy, the last witness of the form: Sophocles's last play, which is also, by historical happenstance, the most recent of the tragedies preserved (but not the last across the board: countless tragedies were subsequently performed in Athens, though all have since been lost).

To confer a particular meaning upon the play for that sole reason would be an error: Sophocles could not imagine that it would become the ultimate specimen of an art form whose actual end would only come a few centuries later.[2] Yet what is false as a historical reality holds a certain truth as a symbol: like it or not, to us *Oedipus at Colonus* is the tomb of Greek tragedy.

It is, indeed, a doubly posthumous work. By 401, the year it was staged, Sophocles had already been dead five years, and tragedy itself was in the process not of dying out, but of changing radically (Aristophanes's *The Frogs* bears witness to this crisis). Perhaps the Ancients were right to choose it as the chronological close of the canon.

Oedipus at Colonus is the other *Oedipus*. In *Oedipus Rex*, the hero who has become the ruler of Thebes sees the monstrous past of which he is the product resurface. Sophocles's final play tells his version of what happened next.[3] Driven out of Thebes with his daughter Antigone, the

---

2   On the other hand, Sophocles could easily sense that this would be the last of his own tragedies and this knowledge may have influenced the composition and meaning of the play. See Chapter 4, 'The God', p. 143.

3   However, the two tragedies are not formally connected, and some have noted inconsistencies between them.

blind and helpless Oedipus arrives by chance in Colonus, a suburb of Athens. After a few incidents, he receives the official hospitality of the Athenians. His wandering life comes to an end, as does his life itself, in miraculous, totally unexplained circumstances. Ultimately, all that is left of Oedipus at Colonus is his tomb, but it is a supernatural tomb, an invisible tomb that cannot be found. It is as inaccessible as Greek tragedy is to us.

What does *this* tragedy without tragedy tell us about tragedy in general? Here are four successive theories – or rather, four enigmas:

- tragedy is a matter of places, to which it is indissolubly bound, and without these places it is (nearly) nothing: a *symbolon* missing its essential half;
- tragedy has nothing to do with what is commonly referred to as tragic: we cannot have a general idea of what it was, what it meant, or the world-view it expressed, because the available corpus is the product of an ideologically biased transmission;
- tragedy had powers inconceivable to us today, such as the power to act upon the audience's bodies and heal them: this is what Aristotle refers to as *catharsis*, a term which must absolutely be restored to its original physiological meaning;
- to represent gods and heroes, tragedy had a religious effectiveness that today must be looked for anywhere but in theatres – perhaps in churches?

The place, the idea, the body, the god: these will be the four sides of this *Tomb of Oedipus*, through which the absolute strangeness of Greek tragedy manifests itself.

Four theories – or four heresies – which go against many a received idea. Four chapters, each of which resonates with episodes of *Oedipus at Colonus*. But also four tributes to scholars and men of letters of centuries past, whose work continues to this day to help us avoid errors always threatening to reappear.

How does Greek tragedy matter to us? In no way: it is totally foreign to us. And so it should be. Yet, against all odds, it continues to move us and change us.

Finally, we will have to explain the mystery of this influence that endures despite so many misunderstandings. For what is at issue here is not to understand tragedy – an impossible task – but rather to fathom the reasons for our inability to understand, to become more aware of who we are.

To learn more about ourselves by what is not us. To grasp *literature* by what is completely out of its grasp. These are the powers of tragedy. And this is its tomb.

Prologue and Parodos

Boundaries and Transgression

An old man shuffles down a road, led by a young woman. In the distance, the ramparts of a city: Athens. The man is called Oedipus, his daughter is Antigone.

He sits down on a rock. A stranger approaches. He tells the travellers that they have arrived in Colonus, an outlying district of Athens, and insistently demands that the old man leave the place, for it is consecrated to the infernal goddesses, the Eumenides. Oedipus refuses: he must first speak to the city's leader.

The stranger leaves to call his fellow citizens. As a precaution, Oedipus and Antigone hide in the forbidden woods. The citizens of Colonus arrive, scandalized to learn that the sanctuary of the Eumenides has been violated.[1] The sight of blind Oedipus coming out of the woods terrifies them. But they are even more horrified when they learn his name, one associated with so many crimes. They repeat their request to Oedipus, accompanied by threats: he must abandon the sanctuary of the Eumenides (otherwise they will refuse to speak to him) and leave the country. Oedipus consents to be led to the edge of the sacred enclosure, but no more: he will not leave Colonus until he has spoken to the king of Athens. Weary, the citizens send for Theseus.

---

1 The moment when the chorus enters is known as *parodos*.

1

The Place

In memoriam Richard Claverhouse Jebb (1841–1905)

Tragedy is a question of places. Defeated Xerxes returns to Susa. Prometheus is chained up in the Caucasus, on the edges of the known world. Victorious Agamemnon comes home to Argos; he will enter the fatal palace despite Cassandra's warnings. Orestes arrives in Athens to be judged. Philoctetes is exiled to the island of Lemnos, where the Greeks will finally have to return to get him. Upon arriving in Aulis, Iphigenia faces her end; miraculously saved, she is taken to Tauris, whence she manages to escape.[1] In every case, the crux of the matter is journeys, exiles, escapes, and returns. Place is the driving force of the drama: it saves the protagonist or sends him to his death. Naturally, other less radical options are possible. Xerxes's return to Susa marks the retreat and isolation in his homeland of the man who had wanted to conquer Greece; rather than triumphing in Athens, he will whimper with his people inside his palace. Here, as in other cases, the place determines the action, the tone and the outcome.

But it is not just any place. It is always a geographical location, which can be located on a map and has a name: town, city-state, locality, mountain, island, and so on – quite

---

1 In these hasty summaries, the reader will have recognized four plays by Aeschylus (*The Persians, Prometheus Bound, Agamemnon, The Eumenides*), one by Sophocles (*Philoctetes*), and two by Euripides (*Iphigenia at Aulis* and *Iphigenia in Tauris*).

unlike the unspecified location that prevails in classical French tragedies, despite the fact that these are directly inspired from the Greek model. The comparison is instructive. The setting of a Racine tragedy is an undefinable space inside a palace: a hallway, vestibule or concourse. A place where people meet, rub shoulders, avoid each other, chase or spy on one another. The setting in Racine is undoubtedly a means of the action, a dramatic tool he puts to use with consummate artfulness. But it is only a neutral place, super-imposed or even more or less identified with the theatrical space, from which it draws all its virtues.

As for the actual geographical setting, it never appears as a driving force of the action – with a few exceptions. The perfect counterexample would be *Bérénice*, in which the foreign queen has to leave Rome against her will – in other words, because of Rome itself. Yet, outside of this remarkable case, the action of Racine's plays could be moved anywhere without causing significant damage. Should a mischievous genie transport Nero's palace to somewhere other than Rome, the characters in *Britannicus* would barely notice: the drama would continue on a similar course whether on the Palatine or in the Indies. Ultimately, it is a palace intrigue and palaces intrigue in the same way wherever they are. Though Phaedra lives in Troezen with her husband Theseus, there is no detail in the play to make this location in any way concrete. Only the sea appears in the distance, but that is not enough to situate the drama – one could just as well be in Athens. Racine's tragedies are rootless, already globalized.

The Stage as Landscape

The situation in fifth-century-BCE tragedy was entirely different, particularly in *Oedipus at Colonus*: the forces driving the action are the very ones traversing and irrigating the space where it is supposed to take place. Perched on the border between two worlds, between the sanctuary and the secular space, having reached an outlying district of Athens without permission to enter the city itself, cast out by both gods and humans, Oedipus appears as the figure of transgression, in other words of the crossing of every boundary: moral, civic and religious. By passing over the divisions between spaces, he makes their ever-present power perceptible and gives form to their immanent presence. Logic or paradox decree that it would take a lame, blind old man to reveal the place and its invisible power.

Yet while the space of Greek tragedy is so energetically structured, it does not have external boundaries. It distinguishes itself from classical French tragedy by its openness: the stage does not represent an enclosed space inside a palace, but an open-air space, a public square – or the edge of woods, as in *Oedipus at Colonus*. The theatre and the setting depicted are perfectly homogenous: the antique stage, which is in the open air, represents a place that is itself under the open sky, while the wings, which the actors access through three doors directly behind the stage, represent an enclosed space (often the interior of a palace), so that there is no difference between the nature of the stage and what it is supposed to show.[2]

To contemporary audiences or theatre makers, such limitations imposed on theatre's powers of representation might seem unbearably irksome. And they would indeed be intolerable had this been theatre in the sense that we understand it today. This was not the case. It would be as absurd to criticize the ancient Greeks for a lack of confidence in theatre's ability to represent everything as it would be to ascribe these

---

2 See Jacques Jouanna's insight on the subject in his admirable summa on Sophocles: *Sophocle* (Paris: Fayard, 2007), 255. See also Lowell Edmunds, *Theatrical Space and Historical Place in Sophocles' Oedipus at Colonus* (Lanham: Rowman & Littlefield, 1996), 39–84.

limitations to a naturalist aesthetic. The very use of the term 'representation' to describe the working of Athenian tragedy is misleading. Perhaps it would be more accurate to refer to 'incarnation' or 'evocation'. Indeed, representation (or *mimesis*, according to Aristotle) implies a symbolic connection between the sign and the reality to which it refers, and introduces a clear division between the order of the signifier and that of the signified. Whereas in the case of evocation or incarnation, something of the aimed-at reality appears in the figuration itself, not as a simple clue or a guarantee of truth, but rather as an effective trace or relic of the real, which therefore becomes directly present – and not represented – on the stage.

In the case of *Oedipus at Colonus*, the power of incarnation is obvious, given that the Theatre of Dionysus, where the play was performed, is located at the foot of the Acropolis in Athens and that the play's action takes place in Athens and its outlying areas. When Antigone enters and says she can see 'the towers crowning the city',[3] she explicitly refers to the Acropolis, which overlooks the theatre and which the audience could see simply by turning around and glancing up. How better to insinuate that the tragedy's action takes place not in a mythical time, the representation of which would only provide a pale copy, but in the here and now of the performance? This is the Greek equivalent of the 'borrowed scenery' (*shakkei*) garden cherished in Japanese tradition: a clearly visible mountain, located outside the garden, far in the distance, is incorporated in the design itself to expand its horizon, inscribe it in the world, and endow it with the cosmic dimension at the heart of any Buddhist garden. The Acropolis therefore rises in the background of *Oedipus at Colonus* like Mount Hiei can be glimpsed in the

---

3 Sophocles, *Oedipus at Colonus*, in *The Three Theban Plays*, trans. Robert Fagles (London: Penguin Books, 1984), v. 15–16. This is the translation used throughout the present text, with occasional modifications where necessary.

distance from various temples in Kyoto, offering a quasi-baroque overspill of reality into the world of figures.

Admittedly, not all the tragedies performed in Athens are supposed to take place in Athens. They cannot all have an element of the Attic landscape directly take part in the drama. But they all unfold under the shared sky of the great human family, a ubiquitous space from which the gods sometimes come down, thanks to some theatre machine. All of these theatre devices name and specifically describe the place where the action happens. In fact, they do more than tell a story that is happening in this place: they remind us of the *history* of the place. Agamemnon is not killed in Argos like any random person; this is not some news clip that could happen as easily here or elsewhere: in the eyes of the Greeks and of eternity, Argos remains Agamemnon's capital, as well as the city where he met a horrible death after ten years of fighting the Trojans. To represent this death is to summon both the place and the hero and to make them present through each other, since it is utterly impossible to separate them. The Greek hero is fundamentally local.

Consequently, there is a necessary link between the space of the stage, on which the drama is performed, and the place evoked: when displayed on stage, the drama allows the mythical place to take shape. And thus during the City Dionysia, when for three days the stage of the Theatre of Dionysus hosted a succession of three tetralogies (in other words, twelve plays featuring up to twelve different locations), Athens became the centre or *omphalos* of the world, in which the founding myths of the Greek city-state and people were recalled and relived. People flocked from all over the Athenian empire, even from all over Greece, to attend this festival: the world descended on the theatre to see itself celebrated in the mirror of the stage.[4]

---

4 On geographic references in tragedy, see André Bernand, *La Carte du tragique: La géographie dans la tragédie grecque* (Paris: Éditions du

In Search of the Lost Place

Yet here comes the inexplicable: tragedy is a question of places, but these places are forever lost to us. The plural is appropriate here, since two places are brought into play in a complementary fashion: the space of the stage and the one in which the myth unfolds. Today all that is left of ancient Greek theatre are relatively uninterpretable remains; we do not even know whether or not the actual stage (or *proskenion*) was raised above the orchestra. As for the mythical places, while their names have miraculously survived on the map, most have disappeared under the dust of history: glorious Mycenae is now but a field of ruins.

The Hellenist Richard Claverhouse Jebb intuited that places were important in tragedy: in his unrivalled edition of *Oedipus at Colonus*, he included a reproduction of a map of Athens featuring the probable location of the story.[5] Any wanderer who enjoys the remains and ghosts of tragedy is infinitely in his debt. But this was in 1886: the place probably still had some of the rural character so palpable in the play.[6] Thirty years later, the academician Paul Girard was already offering a melancholy description of the state of Colonus in his time.[7] Today, Sophocles's native village has

Centre national de la recherche scientifique, 1985). The Panhellenic nature of the performances of the City Dionysia is nicely emphasized in Natale Spineto, *Dionysos a teatro: Il contesto festivo del dramma greco* (Rome: L'Erma di Bretschneider, 2004), 277–92.

5 Sophocles, *The Plays and Fragments, II: The Oedipus Coloneus*, ed. Richard Claverhouse Jebb (Cambridge: Cambridge University Press, 1889 [1st ed., 1886]), xxx.

6 In 1857, the archaeologist Charles Lenormant offered an idyllic description of the landscape of Colonus in 'Œdipe à Colone' au petit séminaire d'Orléans', *Le Correspondant* 41 (1857): 690–1.

7 Paul Girard, 'Au tombeau d'Œdipe', minutes of sessions of the Académie des Inscriptions et Belles-Lettres, 61st year, no. 6, 1917, 433–44 (with photographs).

become a noisy Athens neighbourhood, where only a little public park at the top of the hillock appears to preserve the agrestic charms of the ancient landscape celebrated by the old men of Colonus: in the very place where 'more than elsewhere the nightingale liked best to sing, down in the shadows deepening green, in the wine-dark ivy, in that dense and dark, untrodden, sacred wood of god, rich with laurel and olives never touched by the sun, untouched by storms that blast from every quarter',[8] one now hears nothing but the uninterrupted roar of automobiles, and where the shrine of the Erinyes was once forbidden ground, only the traffic lights endlessly cycling through their luminous litany suggest the slightest prohibition to the passer-by.

If tragedy has lost all its places, can we still hope to understand it? Some will say this is the sad fate of any form of theatre; that, for example, Elizabethan theatre is barely more accessible to us. But, while the stage of the Globe has indeed vanished, numerous documents have preserved its memory, to the point that it recently appeared possible to build a more or less satisfying replica. Four hundred years do infinitely less damage than 4,200 years. Any travellers to Athens who think that they have been transported to the time of Aeschylus and Euripides by standing before the tiered stone seating of the Theatre of Dionysus would be completely wrong: they are primarily admiring the remains of a theatre from the Roman era. The stone theatre itself only dates from the fourth century BCE: at the time of Sophocles, the seating was made of wood. We do not know the exact shape of the orchestra at the time: it may have been rectangular or trapezoidal, but was certainly not the circular shape which we see today.

Yet if that was all, the loss might not seem so important: so many theatres have disappeared over the course of the

---

8 Sophocles, *Oedipus at Colonus*, v. 670–678.

centuries, but their absence has in no way impeded our ability to appreciate the plays that were staged there, nor in some cases to elevate them to the pinnacle of literature. Why would *Ajax* and *Medea* suffer more from the destruction of the stages where they were first performed than *Horace* or *Hamlet*? In fact, they do not and no one has ever considered kicking them or any of the other surviving tragedies of Antiquity out of the canon. Their place at the heart of Western culture seems safe enough.

But is it safe for the right reasons? No matter how gratifying, is not this success the result of deep misunderstanding? Let us be clear. While we should forever be in mourning for the places to which this tragedy was connected, the loss ultimately matters little to us, for it does not prevent us from drawing fulfilling intellectual, aesthetic, and spiritual sustenance from the texts. Fine. But what if that were exactly the problem? What if the intelligibility we thought we were finding in these orphaned works were pure illusion? If, on the contrary, it attested to something else that was lost over the course of these two millennia and that seems impossible ever to bring back? Not the place itself, but in a more fundamental way, the very principle of a connection between text and place; the feeling that a necessary and vital link could exist between a verbal expression and a spatial and geographic situation.

And, so, we read the tragedies like objects detached from their original context of enunciation, stripped of any local reference. According to the scholiast who annotated the manuscript of the play, Athenians were very familiar with the sanctuary of the Eumenides entered by Oedipus, the temple of Demeter where Antigone and Ismene go to fetch water for the ablutions, and especially that so-specifically located place where Oedipus will stop to die – midway between 'the bowl scooped out in the smooth stone where the pact sealed between Theseus and Perithous is cut in stone forever' and 'the Rock of Thoricus', 'the hollow wild-pear', and 'the marble tomb'. Today, the references to these places are totally opaque to us.[9]

At best, we now read them as mere reality effects or, on the contrary, as pure symbols. The latter is the approach taken by Pierre Vidal-Naquet, who identifies in the enumeration of the four points in the centre of which Oedipus will die the subtle structural oppositions between the manufactured and the natural and between life and death.[10] And why not, after all? Anything can be significant. But everything appears all the more significant given that the referent has disappeared. The structuralist interpretation fills the void left by now absent places, now further away from us than any star in the firmament, eroded as they have been by close to two and a half millennia of history.

The Enigma of Oedipus's Double Memorial

Yet the bowl scooped out, the Rock of Thoricus, and the hollow wild-pear were not imaginary places. How can we understand them if we do not know them? No play is more rooted in a distinctive land than *Oedipus at Colonus*.[11] Its subject matter did not come fully formed from Sophocles's creative genius, but was, instead, undoubtedly inspired by a

---

9 Ibid., v. 1590–1603. For the scholia, see the edition provided by August Meineke (Berlin: Weidmann, 1863), 120. The temple of Demeter was probably located on Skouze Hill, where a church now stands, but this is not certain.

10 Pierre Vidal-Naquet, 'Oedipus between Two Cities: An Essay on *Oedipus at Colonus*', in Jean-Pierre Vernant and Pierre Vidal-Naquet, *Myth and Tragedy in Ancient Greece*, trans. Janet Lloyd (New York: Zone Books, 1988), 358.

11 See Reginald Pepys Winnington-Ingram, *Sophocles: An Interpretation* (Cambridge: Cambridge University Press, 1980), 339–40; Charles Segal, *Tragedy and Civilization: An Interpretation of Sophocles* (Cambridge, MA: Harvard University Press, 1981), 404.

local legend, particularly given that the story took place in the writer's native deme: all it would have taken was an altar dedicated to the hero, an inscription at the sanctuary of the Eumenides, or a phrase spoken in a ritual.

In the second century AD, Pausanias reports the existence in Colonus of 'a hero shrine [*heroon*] of Perithous and Theseus and Oedipus and Adrastos'.[12] He does not see any enclosure dedicated to the Erinyes; however, he describes a sanctuary of the Eumenides near the Aeropagos, containing 'a monument to Oedipus' – or even his 'tomb', for the term used (*mnêma*) is ambiguous.[13] The geographer does not hide the dilemma he faces regarding the monument next to the Aeropagos: while the tradition according to which Oedipus died in Colonus is well attested prior to Sophocles's play,[14] how to explain the presence of another monument within the city itself? 'After diligent inquiry' (*polupragmonôn*), Pausanias finally 'finds' that Oedipus's bones were allegedly brought to Athens from Thebes. The oratory precautions taken and the vague term used (*polupragmonein*) lead one to believe that this is not a case of a tradition duly attested to and brought to light by the scholar, but a purely personal hypothesis based on a passage from the *Iliad* stating that Oedipus died in Thebes.[15] Nothing suggests we should accept Pausanias's debatable hypothesis, which certainly

---

12 Pausanias, *Guide to Greece, Vol. I: Central Greece*, trans. Peter Levi (London: Penguin Books, 1979), 89; see *Description of Greece* (I, 30, 4).

13 Pausanias, *Description of Greece, Vol. I*, trans. W. H. S. Jones (Cambridge, MA: Harvard University Press, Loeb Classical Library, 1918), 141 (I, 28, 7). Here, I diverge from both the English and French translations (Pausanias, *Description de la Grèce*, trans. Jean Pouilloux [Paris: Belles Lettres, 1992]), as well as the commentary by François Chamoux in the French edition, 224. At the beginning of the first century AD, Valerius Maximus (V, 3) also mentions the existence of an 'altar' (*ara*) built on the 'bones' (*ossa*) of Oedipus and located between the Aeropagos and the Acropolis.

14 See Euripides, *The Phoenicians*, v. 1706–1707, unless, of course, these verses were interpolated later.

15 Homer, *Iliad*, XXIII, v. 678–680, cited by Pausanias, *Description of Greece*.

contradicts Sophocles's play: rather than a 'tomb', the *mnêma* could simply be a 'memorial' or a 'cenotaph'.

If the two monuments at Colonus and in Athens itself already existed in Sophocles's time, the playwright conceivably chose to merge them in a single plot by having Oedipus stop in a sanctuary of the Eumenides resembling the one by the Aeropagos, but located in Colonus. Unless theatre served as a model for reality: since the tragedy describes how the Theban exile placed himself under the protection of the Erinyes, the play could have inspired the erection of a memorial to Oedipus in the principal Athenian sanctuary dedicated to the Eumenides, which was the one located between the Aeropagos and the Acropolis.[16] This sanctuary within striking distance of the Theatre of Dionysus, so emphatically celebrated by Aeschylus in his *Oresteia*, had already made, after all, a significant impact on the genre of tragedy. In which case Sophocles's play would have had the power to exert an effect on the real, even to create it, by fashioning it in its own image.[17] Stemming from geographic space, it would have modified it in return, the way that the village of Illiers, in the French department of Eure-et-Loir, was recently inspired by Marcel Proust to take the mythical name of Combray.

---

16 Lenormant expressed a similar idea in '*Œdipe à Colone*', 709: 'People could not even agree on the place where Oedipus's ashes rested. While the poet claimed them for his native village, others carried them to the foot of the Acropolis, on the Aeropagos hill, next to the other sanctuary of the Eumenides, and this double attribution was not shocking in and of itself, since ultimately, it was a single symbol, whose only historical aspect was its origin, and which could arouse the same veneration in two different places.'

17 For a well-researched discussion on the location of Oedipus's tomb, see Emily Kearns, *The Heroes of Attica* (London: Institute of Classical Studies, 1989), 208–9. However, the hypothesis I suggest is not mentioned.

There Is No Greek *Literature*

Greek tragedy, and particularly *Oedipus at Colonus*, is singularly located. One might think that in this it only enjoys the privilege of the genre to which it belongs. By definition, in so far as representation imposes a relationship to space, no literary production is more specifically located than theatre – to such an extent that there is now a strong tendency to place this genre on the margins of literature, if not simply outside of it. The signs of this gradual marginalization are obvious: it is probably no coincidence that, today, drama teaching in universities is increasingly confined to performing arts departments designed for that purpose, and forsaken by strictly literary courses.

Conversely, while certain recent critical approaches are open to literature's geographic dimension,[18] it would, on the face of it, seem inconceivable to make place the essential parameter of any literary object – not only theatre – for the specific reason that what we generally call *literature*, in the modern sense of the term, is any form of verbal expression that extends beyond the particular space of its enunciation. According to this common understanding of the word, literature is defined by its timeless currency and the fact that it is delocalized: when a text achieves literary dignity, it somehow escapes the conditions of its production and encounters an audience other than that which had initially been anticipated. Texts that are generally not read outside of their original context, such as instruction manuals and satirical tracts, have no chance of being literature. They can certainly be read centuries later as historical documents, but as such

---

18 See Franco Moretti, *Atlas of the European Novel 1800–1900* [1997] (London: Verso, 1998); Bertrand Westphal, *La Géocritique* (Paris: Éditions de Minuit, 2007).

they continue to refer back to their context. Conversely, when we categorize *Les Provinciales* as a literary object due to its intrinsic aesthetic qualities, we simply mean that we can enjoy reading the text regardless of its historical framework, without being deeply passionate about the quarrels between Jesuits and Jansenists (though one should be, just a little). One could go so far as to say that pure literature – the novel, poetry – is equivalent to an absolute deterritorialization.

Yet, while it is true that Greek tragedy is determined by its relationship to space, this relationship is far from specific to it in the context of ancient literature. In ancient Greece, everything we now call *literature* had a special relationship to place – not necessarily a geographical place but, first, an enunciative one: a Greek work always displays its origin. The oldest literary texts are statements with perfectly explicit parameters, uttered by a speaker who stands at the front of the stage, addressed to an audience no less clearly indicated.[19] Homer and Hesiod invoke the Muses in order to let them speak through their mouths. Herodotus gives public readings of his *Histories*. Pindar dedicates his songs to the winners of the Olympic Games, Sappho to her male and female lovers. Plato develops his thinking through a conversational – or embodied – form. These texts that have reached us only in their written form were initially conceived to be read out loud, recited, or sung.

Given these conditions, theatre appeared less of an exception than it does today. Theatre was not distinguished from other genres by the fact that it was performed, for all other texts of the period were likewise intended for performance. The real specificity of the theatrical form was in its recourse to alterity: the speakers did not speak in their own name, but while wearing the mask of a character.

---

19 See Bruno Gentili, *Poesia e pubblico nella Grecia antica* (Rome: Laterza, 1989).

Greek theatre therefore functioned in exactly the opposite way to our contemporary theatre. Today, written texts, which we access in silence, tend to function as statements without speakers, removed from the conditions of their production, while plays find most of their power in an embodied, flesh-and-bone speaker. The written text takes shape in an absence, theatre does so in a presence: at any rate, this is how things stand today. In ancient Greece, it was the contrary: while every text did have a recognized speaker – as in our contemporary theatre – tragedy literally masked and disguised the speaker, making him invisible in order to allow another type of presence to emerge. In Greek theatre, the speaker withdrew to make way for someone else, the *character*: god, hero, or human. A disappearance took place, immediately followed by an appearance. The covering of one figure coincided with the unveiling of another and led to a double displacement, in terms of both space and identity: into a place and into a character. Nietzsche suggests the Dionysian frenzy had the ability to erase the boundaries between individualities and encourage the crossing of appearances: the Greek theatre was the place where one became absent from one's self and another world emerged.[20]

The relationship between theatre and literature in the fifth century BCE was, therefore, the opposite of the one that exists today, when it is the written text that seems like a mask placed on the real, and the novel whose function is to create worlds. How are we to understand a system so different, one that so radically transforms our ways of reading, seeing and thinking? Naturally, one may attempt to conceptualize this entire way of functioning, as we are trying to do now, by studying the texts, looking for contemporary accounts, and considering the archaeological record. But the

---

20 See Jean-Pierre Vernant, 'The God of Tragic Fiction' [1981], in Vernant and Vidal-Naquet, *Myth and Tragedy in Ancient Greece*, 181.

concept only allows us to outline the contours of the thing; it does not allow us to enter. Will we have to be satisfied with staying on the threshold?

An Analogy: Noh

One of the principal obstacles to the study of Greek theatre is that we do not know the conditions under which performance took place. No doubt many scholars dream of some benevolent god transporting them to fifth-century-BCE Athens to witness even a single day of the City Dionysia. This would resolve countless problems at a stroke, given how much of the material reality of these performances escapes us. But it would also raise countless new and far more complex questions, of which no one currently has any inkling. Speculation on the nature of Greek theatre would hardly be simplified. On the contrary.

This dream is all the more absurd since its fulfilment would probably create more obscurity than it would dissipate. Yet it is nonetheless significant in that it models itself on the very object it claims to reveal: as we have seen, the system of tragedy consists precisely of fitting a presence over an absence, of making another reality emerge by removing real life. As described and seen from the outside, this mechanism that is nothing other than fantasy itself can only frustrate the contemporary scholar forced to consider it with the required epistemological distance, without participating in the performance. The mechanism therefore calls for an intensification of the fantasy that would lead the scholar finally to surmount their own psychological and cultural defences and see the materiality of theatre appear in all its spectacular power. An infinite unveiling, needlessly repeated, by which the illusion of a performance would follow the performance of an illusion. But so long as the system of tragedy is only considered from an external perspective, it cannot be otherwise: the cold and objective description of Greek theatre – or rather of what we know of it – can only lead to frustration and incomprehension, and this frustration demands to be overcome by whatever means necessary. Dreaming would be one approach. Are there others?

What about analogy? While it does not enable us miraculously to penetrate the mystery of a lost reality, it at least makes perceptible the distance that remains to be travelled, the level of culture shock which anyone who wishes to comprehend the singularity of a vanished cultural event must necessarily experience.

As it happens, 2,000 years later and a little over 6,000 miles from Athens, a theatrical form appeared that shared numerous characteristics with Greek tragedy: the exclusive participation of male actors, the wearing of masks, the presence of a chorus, the use of music, song and dance, the strong ritual dimension, and even the organization of the performance into complete days that include farces – to mention only the most obvious elements.[21] And the miracle, if indeed there is a miracle, is that this theatrical form still exists today and that anyone can attend a performance in conditions very similar to those that originally prevailed. Not that such an experience allows us to make convenient inferences from one form of theatre to the other. It is primarily valuable for the powerful culture shock to which it exposes the viewer. It allows questioning and hypothesis.[22]

Most importantly, this shift provides an opportunity to encounter another form of theatre that is largely characterized

---

21 For a comparison of tragedy and Noh, see Mae J. Smethurst, *The Artistry of Aeschylus and Zeami: A Comparative Study of Greek Tragedy and No* (Princeton, NJ: Princeton University Press, 1989); Jason Roussos, 'Ancient Greek Tragedy and Noh', *Diotima* 13 (1985): 121–8.

22 This method of comparison was described by Marcel Detienne, *Comparer l'incomparable* [2000] (Paris: Seuil, 2009).

by its grounding in a geographic space. It is certainly paradoxical to have to search so far and so late for this example of a theatre putting down roots, in a way nearly contradictory with what we seek to illustrate, but the space in and of itself is far less important than the relationship to space, which can remain identical despite the variability of place. This is the case with Noh, a theatrical form that appeared in the Japanese archipelago in the fourteenth century AD, a long way from our own century and even further from that of Aeschylus, Sophocles and Euripides. Yet the tradition of Noh has been maintained with surprising continuity: to this day, performances are produced by the same families that originally did so.

These are plays featuring little text and in which the action is limited to an absolute minimum. A typical Noh play, known as a 'ghost Noh', generally follows a structure in two timeframes.[23] An itinerant monk, played by an actor not wearing a mask, arrives in a given place; he meets a strange person, a woman or an old man, played by a masked actor, then this character leaves. End of the first part, followed by an interlude: an inhabitant of the region appears, a simple farmer played by an unmasked actor who specializes in farce; questioned by the monk, the villager initially pretends not to know anything, out of politeness, then explains in great detail that the strange character was probably the ghost of a bygone hero or the apparition of a local god. This interlude gives the masked actor time to change his costume and appearance. In the second half, after the monk has prayed for the salvation of the hero or the blessing of the god, the character from the first part reappears in his supernatural form, performs a dance, then leaves, having

---

23 I am summarizing the typical plot of a so-called supernatural or ghost Noh play (*mugen noh*), leaving aside the present-day or real-world Noh (*genzai noh*), of which there are far fewer examples and which are a little more similar to our usual theatrical dramas.

potentially been saved or falling back into his hell. End of the Noh.

It would be difficult to make anything simpler. But it is equally difficult to do justice in such a brief summary to the richness and poetic complexity of these plays, rivalling the Greek tragedies in terms of verbal beauty and emotional power – though they use very different dramatic devices.

In fact, there is no drama, strictly speaking. Paul Claudel said as much in a brutal but not inaccurate statement: 'Drama is something that happens, Noh is someone who arrives.'[24] One could add: Noh is someone who arrives, because something has *already* happened. The action of a ghost Noh has already taken place, long ago. The play's function is to describe this action in three different and successive forms: a first time, made of fragments and enigmatic allusions, when the monk meets the strange character; a second time, in the interlude, in the most prosaic, flattest way possible, through the villager's words; and a third and final time through a performance enhanced by transfiguration and dance. In a way, the second part presents a retrospective vision in the form of a dream, in which the interlocutor, who has remained on stage, sees the divine, demonic, or spectral reality of the human being whom he met earlier; now transfigured, this character reveals his true supernatural identity or the incarnation that determined his karma. It is hard to know whether the apparition in the second part is real or part of a dream, but this may not really matter, since, according to Buddhism, which provides much of the ideological framework for Noh, the world is but an illusion. In any case, Noh offers anything but the linear

---

24 Paul Claudel, 'Nô', in *Œuvres en prose* (Paris: Gallimard, 'Bibliothèque de la Pléiade', 1965), 1167. [Translator's note: Claudel's French plays on the double meaning of the verb 'arriver', both 'to arrive' and 'to happen'. 'Le drame, c'est quelque chose qui arrive, le nô, c'est quelqu'un qui arrive.']

unfolding of a plot: in Noh, everything has already taken place, and it is our vision that changes.

Everything has already taken place, and, in fact, all that remains is the place, sole witness to the vanished past, the fleeting encounters and illusory perceptions whose ephemeral reunion will constitute the Noh play over the course of a performance. Each of the stories remembered by the Noh is connected to a clearly defined place. One could draw up a precise map of the location described in a Noh play, particularly since many of the sites concerned still feature a memorial dedicated to the stories' main character. These come in the form of a Shinto sanctuary, an altar lost in the woods, or a simple stone stele covered in moss. In a suburb west of Kobe, one can still see the stump of the pine under which two sisters, Pining Wind and Autumn Rain, waited in vain for their lost lover. In Miho, in Shizuoka Prefecture, it is said that a pine now protected by a fence is the one on which a daughter of the Sky hung her feather mantle – even though the original tree was lost in 1707 following the eruption of Mount Fuji. In Isonokami, in the south of Nara, the construction of a new road paved over a well next to which a child met her future husband, Narihira, and which she was unable to leave now that she had become a ghost. Luckily a brand-new well has been placed right beside it, for modern Japanese society goes to great lengths to care for its ghosts and their comfort.[25] There are many other examples. The origin of these various memorials is not as clear: the Noh plays were sometimes less inspired *by* the memorials and more inspiring *of* them. But the memorial is secondary; it was preceded by the legend, and there is no question that every Noh play celebrates a place and the legendary figure that haunts it.

---

25 The allusions here are to three of the most famous Noh plays, respectively: *Matsukaze*, *Hagoromo*, and *Izutsu*. See Royall Tyler, *Japanese No Dramas* (London: Penguin, 1992), 191, 100 and 123.

Oedipus in Kyoto

If Colonus had been a suburb not of Athens but of Kyoto, it is very likely that one would still find a temple dedicated to Oedipus there. This idea is not as absurd as it may seem, for to the east of the former Japanese capital, near the city of Otsu, there is a Shinto sanctuary devoted to a blind prince who is said to have lived out his final days in exile on a nearby mountain, more than 1,000 years ago. This prince lent his name to a famous Noh play attributed to the great Zeami (1363–1443). While the prince in question is not Oedipus, of course, there are ample coincidences between the story of the fallen king of Thebes and that of Semimaru.

The action takes place in the tenth century during the reign of Emperor Daigo, on Mount Osaka, east of Kyoto.[26] An officer of the court is commanded to abandon the emperor's son, Prince Semimaru, who was born blind, in the mountains. He leads him there under escort. Once they have reached their destination, he cuts the prince's hair, removes his beautiful brocade garments and turns him into a monk, leaving him only his lute. Wearing a modest straw coat and a hat to protect himself from the rain, Semimaru is now alone. During the interlude, a courtier seized with pity for the poor prince comes to build him a hut. In the second part, a madwoman appears wandering through the mountains, her hair weirdly standing straight up: this is Princess Sakagami, a daughter of the emperor, who has also been cast out of the palace, because she is mad. She stops by the thatched hut, hears Semimaru's voice singing as he accompanies himself on the lute, and opens the door: brother and sister recognize each other and fall into each other's arms in tears.

---

26 Mount Osaka should not be confused with the metropolis of the same name, which is located to the south of the former capital.

For a few minutes they bemoan their fate together, but the time to separate soon arrives. Sakagami must return to her mad wandering. The play ends with the chorus singing a song that describes the scene as it takes place:

> 'Farewell', she calls to him, and he responds,
> 'Please visit me as often as you can.'
> (*Sakagami walks toward the wings and turns back.*)
> Her voice grows faint but still he listens
> (*Sakagami starts to exit. Semimaru takes a few steps
> forward, stops and listens.*
> *He turns his head toward the princess.*)
> She turns a final time to look at him.
> (*Sakagami stops and looks off in the distance*)
> Weeping, weeping they have parted,
> Weeping, weeping they have parted.
> (*Sakagami exits into the wings, making the gesture of
> weeping; Semimaru executes the same gesture, having
> stayed alone on stage.*)[27]

Few moments are as heart-rending as this final separation, particularly since no explanation is offered for this sudden departure as mysterious as the initial encounter between brother and sister. This mystery is also one of the potential parallels with *Oedipus at Colonus*: nothing is ever properly explained about Oedipus's fate, which consists, once he has arrived as an exile in Athens, in his meeting in rapid succession all the members of his family whom he thought he had left behind in Thebes, then dying in supernatural circumstances. The only justification given is derived from oracles, but an oracle, in and of itself, does not offer an explanation; it is the

---

27 Zeami, *Semimaru*, in *Twenty Plays of the No Theatre*, trans. Donald Keene, ed. Susan Matisoff (New York: Columbia University Press, 1970), 112. I have adapted the stage directions provided by the translator.

verbal expression of a fate whose true cause remains impenetrable. The oracle simply states the fact that the gods have decided it must be so: it sanctifies the arbitrariness of existence.

The cause of Semimaru's misfortunes is scarcely clearer. When the officer tasked with abandoning him begins to express outrage at having to carry out such an unjust order, the prince immediately stops him:

> I was born blind because I was lax in my religious duties in a
>   former life.
> That is why the Emperor, my father,
> Ordered you to leave me in the wilderness,
> Heartless this would seem, but it's his plan
> To purge in this world my burden from the past,
> And spare me suffering in the world to come.
> This is a father's true kindness.
> You should not bewail his decree.[28]

While exile is supposed to allow the prince to atone, by living ascetically, for mistakes made in a past life, the transgression itself remains unknown. Similarly, the unlikely meeting of the brother and sister is explained in a beautiful Buddhist adage which the characters cite on two occasions: two people need only have sheltered from the rain together beneath a single tree for their karmas to be forever connected in their present and future incarnations.[29] This belief certainly justifies the idea that a brother and sister could unexpectedly find each other despite their exile, lost in the mountains after their paths have separated. But it also opens a dizzying perspective on the past, raising new questions that remain unanswered. In particular, it does not explain exactly why Semimaru and Sakagami are brother and sister; it says nothing of what

---

28 Ibid., 104.
29 Ibid., 110, 111. See also note 16, p. 114.

THE PLACE

created a strong enough connection between their karmas in a past life to cause them to be born into the same family.

Goodbye, Aristotle

The play's audience can therefore have the legitimate impression not just of tragic events unfolding before their eyes, but of witnessing the distant consequences of other tragic events in which the characters' past incarnations were involved, and about which no one will ever learn anything. There is no action, only indirect repercussions of a past action that remains forever unknown. From this perspective, while it is not strictly speaking a ghost Noh, a play like *Semimaru* features a similar decentring of the plot: the actual drama takes place elsewhere than on stage, in a distant past that does not coincide with the time of the performance.

The same is true of Oedipus: the misfortunes that afflict him proceed from causes that predate his own existence. Ismene mentions 'the old familial calamity (*genous*) that weighs on [this] long-suffering house'. Oedipus himself refers to 'the pleasure of the gods, raging against [his] family (*genos*) probably for such a long time'.[30] What is the cause of this calamity? It is never properly elucidated. The allusion is naturally to the oracles who told Laius that 'he would die at the hands of his children'.[31] But these oracles seem equally arbitrary. Do we need to look further back? Struck by the unexplained nature of these misfortunes, many commentators suggest a family curse due to the transgression Laius committed when he abducted Chrysippus, the son of his host Pelops, to have carnal relations with him; Laius was thus credited with inventing same-sex intercourse. The

30 Sophocles, *Oedipus at Colonus*, v. 369–370, 964–965.
31 Ibid., v. 970.

25

problem is that this theory rests upon pure conjecture by modern-day scholars, speculating on lost plays by Euripides; in fact, there is no surviving ancient text in which Laius's act is explicitly considered the source of the curse on the Labdacids.[32] The exact origin of Oedipus's misfortunes remains as enigmatic as that of Semimaru's: both plays only refer to distant causes the better to obscure their nature. The modern scholar, keen to maintain the rationality of cause and effect, is forced to come up with hypotheses.

Perhaps the scholar is simply misguided in wanting to force onto these plays an aetiological framework derived from his or her own agenda, but not suited to the plays' actual nature. Influenced by an entire Aristotelian tradition of theatre and fiction criticism, we indeed tend to want Noh and tragedy to present the whole of an action, complete in and of itself and with all the reasoning to go with it. Aristotle insists on this point several times:

> Now, according to our definition, Tragedy is an imitation of an action that is complete, and whole . . . A whole is that which has a beginning, a middle, and an end. A beginning is that which does not itself follow anything by causal necessity, but after which something naturally is or comes to be. An end, on the contrary, is that which itself naturally follows some other thing, either by necessity, or probability, but has nothing following it. A middle is that which follows something as some other things follow it. A well-constructed plot, therefore, must neither begin nor end haphazardly, but conform to these principles.[33]

---

32   This theory is developed by Hugh Lloyd-Jones, *The Justice of Zeus* (Berkeley: University of California Press, 1971), 120–2, and discussed by Jean Bollack, *La Naissance d'Œdipe: Traduction et commentaires d'Œdipe roi* (Paris: Gallimard, 1995), 256–7.

33   Aristotle, *Poetics*, trans. S. H. Butcher (New York: Hill and Wang, 1961), 65 (VII, 50 b 21–34). I have slightly altered the translation. See also 67 (VIII, 51 a 30–35).

It is clear that *Semimaru* does not fit this Aristotelian definition of a complete action. The beginning of the play, as I
have said, is the necessary consequence of a cause that is
never made clear; the middle produces a princess who has never
been mentioned previously; and her departure, as unexplained as her arrival, does not offer a satisfying end.
Semimaru therefore does not fit into the framework of
Aristotelian poetics. It is true that Aristotle made no claim to
theorizing Noh theatre, but one might have expected, after
all, that a concept as general as that of complete action could
apply without too much difficulty even to a Japanese play.
That is not the case.

Does *Oedipus at Colonus* better fit the mould? It seems
unlikely. We have seen the extent to which the play's action
is dependent on causes taking place much earlier than the
actual beginning of the tragedy, some of which are perfectly
explicit (Oedipus's crimes and exile), while others – the most
fundamental – are left unsaid (the origin of the curse on the
Labdacids). Additionally, the succession of episodes does
not follow the rule of necessity: commentators have long
criticized, with all due respect to Sophocles, the disjointed
nature of a play presenting a succession of unrelated appearances (Ismene, Creon, Polynices).[34] One might think that the
denouement, at least, would avoid such criticism: this is not
exactly the case. Yes, Oedipus's death puts an end to his own
misfortunes. But it very explicitly sparks the sequence of
calamities fated to descend upon the Labdacids: the frat-
ricidal war between Eteocles and Polynices and Antigone's
revolt. It would probably be excessive to conclude that the
play is incoherent, given that the plot does follow a certain
temporal logic and that there are obviously no surrealist-style

---

34 See, for example, R. C. Jebb in the introduction to his edition of
Oedipus at Colonus, xliii–xliv. See also Kathleen Freeman, 'The Dramatic
Technique of the *Oedipus Coloneus*', *The Classical Review* 37, nos 3–4
(May–June 1923): 50–4; Winnington-Ingram, *Sophocles*, 248.

incongruities. But the various scenes are nonetheless connected to each other in the loosest of fashions. If *Semimaru* fails to satisfy the criteria of coherence and wholeness spelled out by Aristotle, *Oedipus at Colonus* does not score much higher.

Should this really bother us? Should we join certain recent critics in striving to defend Sophocles against each of these charges, point by point?[35] Or is it, rather, a case of the Aristotelian reading of theatre showing its limitations here, including when it comes to tragedy?[36] In other words, perhaps we are asking the wrong questions of these plays when we seek to read them as statements on the causes and effects of actions. This is not where the essential aim of these performances lies.

At Mount Osaka

Where, then, does it lie? Precisely in the relationship to place, which provides a significant part of the action's narrative thread. As strange as it may seem at first glance, the dramatic coherence of these works is largely found in parameters apparently external to them, or even completely heterogeneous. Does this seem difficult to accept? Probably, but only because we are unable to conceive of a literary text achieving its unity elsewhere than within itself, that is to say, elsewhere than within an ideological and aesthetic framework of which the text itself lays all the foundations. So that

35 See, notably, Andreas Markantonatos, *Oedipus at Colonus: Sophocles, Athens, and the World* (Berlin: De Gruyter, 2007), 121–3.

36 On this subject, see the fundamental essay by Florence Dupont, *Aristote ou le vampire du théâtre occidental* (Paris: Flammarion, 2007). The incompatibility of *Oedipus at Colonus* with the Aristotelian categories had earlier been noted by Eleftheria A. Bernidaki-Aldous, *Blindness in a Culture of Light: Especially the Case of Oedipus at Colonus of Sophocles* (New York: Peter Lang, 1990), 215–16, 229–30.

even if, by some slim chance, we were able to take into account this exteriority of the work, such a mechanism would doubtless strike us as an unforgivable aesthetic weakness. Yet this is exactly how a play like *Semimaru* functions, with a plot that is intimately linked to the legends and religious cults specific to Mount Osaka. Let us get specific and do what is required of us, which is to dive into certain details that are ostensibly anything but literary. To travellers who wanted to leave the capital heading east, the mountain provided a convenient pass: this was the first stage on the famous Tōkaidō Road. To this day, a railway line and a heavily congested road follow the route; there is even a tunnel named Semimaru, in the latest manifestation of the local legend popularized by Zeami's play. But the pass was no less crowded in the fourteenth century and earlier eras: the custom at the time was to accompany travellers up to the barrier marking the boundary of the capital's territory and to say farewell here; people also came to the barrier to meet those returning from a long trip. A poem by the real Semimaru describes the constant traffic at the pass:

> This, now this!
> Where people come and people go
> For friends and strangers alike
> This is Meeting Barrier.[37]

The poem is partially cited in the play.[38] In fact, poetic conventions had very early made Osaka the emblematic location for every meeting, which was a natural evolution

---

37 'Kore ya kono / Yuku mo kaeru mo / Wakaretsutsu / Shirumo shiranu mo / Ausaka no seki.' Poem 951 of the *Gosenshû*, quoted by Susan Matisoff, *The Legend of Semimaru, Blind Musician of Japan* (New York: Columbia University Press, 1978), 163. The translation is based on one by Donald Keene, lightly altered by Susan Matisoff.

38 Zeami, *Semimaru*, 275.

given that according to its original spelling, the name meant 'the hill of reunion' (*Ausaka*). At least as early as the tenth century, a Shinto sanctuary was built here in honour of Sakagami, whose name literally means 'the deity of the hill'. People later came here to honour the memory of a more or less mythical poet, Semimaru, whom an entire corporation of nomadic musician priests had adopted as their patron. The association of Sakagami and Semimaru in the same religious cult came all the more easily given that it was traditional in Japan to go to mountain passes to venerate a couple composed of a male and a female deity, who may have corresponded to the mountain's two opposite slopes.[39]

In these few geographical details, we find all the material for the play. The influence of the Indian Buddhist legend of blind Prince Kunala, who is expelled from the palace and then recognized through his musical gifts, quickly identifies Semimaru as a son of the emperor.[40] The Osaka Barrier provides the rest, that is to say the general theme: a series of farewells and reunions on the mountain. Farewell to Semimaru, who abandons Kyoto and the luxury of the imperial palace. Reunion with Sakagami, immediately followed by another farewell. Indeed, the princess's departure has no other justification than to illustrate the Osaka Barrier's function, as described in the famous Semimaru poem quoted above: 'Where people come and people go / For friends and strangers alike.' This is a delicate metaphor for the impermanence of valued things in Buddhist doctrine, but also a Shinto symbol of the two slopes of the pass, both united and separate. This kind of syncretism of Shintoism and Buddhism is typical of Japanese religion.

---

39 For further details, see the highly informed work of Matisoff, *Legend of Semimaru*, 3–54.
40 *Konjaku monogatari* (IV, 4), quoted in ibid., 168–72.

Zeami's brilliant invention was to turn the deity of the mountain, who is venerated as half of the couple she forms with Semimaru, into a sister of the prince, enabling the connection between the play's second part and the first, with each part focused on the farewell to friends and family. But Sakagami's conspicuous madness, which also serves as a paradoxically rational justification for her sudden departure, confers upon the character an aura and a supernatural dimension that bring her closer to her original divine status. Without explicitly stating as much, Zeami uses the play to describe how Semimaru and Sakagami became the two guardian deities of the Osaka Barrier: having reached every level of Buddhist perfection, they are gods or *kami* in the making. Indeed, according to the syncretic theory prevalent from the end of the Heian period, *kami* in Shinto are merely the local manifestations of Buddhas and Bodhisattvas.[41] The Noh play *Semimaru* stages the origins of the cult practised at the sanctuary on Mount Osaka in a singularly concise manner.

Zeami's play is incomprehensible – or close to it – if we do not consider it through the lens of its essential relationship to the place it claims to illustrate. But it does more than illustrate it: it finds roots, meaning, and purpose there. It is inseparable from it.

In the Attic Countryside

It should be possible to say the same about *Oedipus at Colonus*. Unfortunately, in this instance, time has done its destructive work. There is practically nothing left of the

---

41 This is the *honji suijaku* theory. See Mark Teeuwen and Fabio Rambelli, eds, *Buddhas and Kami in Japan: Honji Suijaku as a Combinatory Paradigm* (London: Routledge Curzon, 2003).

THE TOMB OF OEDIPUS

places mentioned in the tragedy: after our successful pilgrimage to the mountain outside Kyoto, our hike through the Attic countryside is likely to disappoint. Even the memory of the places only survives in a few scattered and fragmentary texts, which, like those by Pausanias, are not always reliable. One thing is certain, however: the play stages the origins of the hero cult of Oedipus in the small rustic town of Colonus. Numerous details in the text will forever remain incomprehensible to us because they are linked to vanished elements of the landscape and to monuments and local traditions of which any memory has been lost for centuries. There is very little we can still grasp.

It is not impossible, for example, that the parade of different characters who come to meet Oedipus, and whose somewhat incongruous succession has so often been criticized, was justified by some distinctive feature of the cult practised at Colonus, much as Sakagami's appearance in *Semimaru* can be explained by the nature of the deities worshipped at the Osaka Barrier. But we have to resign ourselves to perpetual ignorance: we cannot pretend that the place has not been lost. The field is therefore left open to interpretation and conjecture.

Exegetes have often raised one specific hypothesis: that the arrival of all these Thebans on the outskirts of Athens could be linked to an episode of the Peloponnesian War, which was then recent enough for the play's audience to have it in mind. Around 407, the Athenians had succeeded in repelling an assault by the Theban cavalry in the area of Colonus.[42] The tragedy appears to allude to this event when

---

42 See Diodorus Siculus, *Library of History*, XIII, 72, cited by Markantonatos, *Oedipus at Colonus*, 149. It was also in Colonus that an extraordinary session of the people's assembly was held in 411, putting an end to the democratic regime. According to Jouanna (*Sophocle*, 60), Sophocles may well have wanted to exorcize the memory of that unhappy event through his play. This hypothesis does not invalidate the previous one for, as so often in literary and artistic creation, an author's choices may be overdetermined.

Oedipus tells Theseus that his tomb would keep the city 'safe from the ravages of the men sprung up from the sowing',[43] in other words, safe from the Thebans, who were said to have sprung up from the dragon's teeth sowed by Cadmus. The arguments against Creon and Polynices clearly stem from the same intention: against the tyrant who wants to expel him from Athens and against his son who asks him for a blessing, the old blind man asserts his unswerving attachment to his new adoptive city and his hostility to anything from Thebes. Alive, he repels the Thebans as victoriously as he will once dead. This interpretation can be confirmed by a late scholium according to which Oedipus appeared to encourage the Athenians to resist the Thebans during an unspecified battle.[44] But let us not rush to embrace this scholium, nor draw too many definitive conclusions from it: the scholium might only be a consequence of the influence of Sophocles's play.

However much we want to, we cannot escape this impasse: without the places, our reading of the tragedy will forever remain patchy and incomplete. Which naturally brings to mind the moment when Oedipus, wanting to keep secret the location of his tomb, asks Theseus to remain silent about it:

> [You] alone must keep [this mystery] safe forever, and when
> you reach the end of your own life, entrust it to the worthiest,
> so that he reveal [it] to his heir and so on through the gener-
> ations, on forever.[45]

Over the course of the plot, this mystery surrounding the tomb is initially connected to the hope of turning it into a

---

43 Sophocles, *Oedipus at Colonus*, v. 1533-1534.
44 Scholium on Aelius Aristides, *In Defense of the Four* (172, 1), ed. Wilhelm Dindorf (Leipzig: Weidmann, 1829), vol. 3, 560, cited by Markantonatos, *Oedipus at Colonus*, 149.
45 Sophocles, *Oedipus at Colonus*, v. 1530-1532.

defence against the Thebans: it is absolutely essential that they be prevented from moving the tomb or visiting it to carry out sacrifices, which would oblige the buried hero to favour them.[46] It is even entirely plausible that this passage alludes to a genuine tradition, related to a cult practised in Colonus and known to the audience.

On the other hand, we could also see this mystery as a simple attempt to be realistic: if the play's Athenian audience had never heard that Oedipus died at Colonus, it was prudent on the part of the playwright to prepare them for the surprise. The secrecy Oedipus maintained around the location of his grave would then neatly justify this general ignorance.

Though contradictory, both interpretations are possible. How to choose between them? Now that every document has vanished, that all the sites have changed radically and all the traditions have been erased, today's readers are left to trust their intuition. What was not ambiguous at the time the plays were initially staged has now become so.

Portrait of Tragedy as the Winged Victory of Samothrace

The most paradoxical aspect of all this is that the new ambiguity, due solely to our ignorance and the disappearance of the play's whole historical and geographical context, can now be seen as something that enriches the work. Polysemy is indeed commonly regarded as a characteristic of literary utterance, not to say as a principal indicator of their very literariness. The more potential meanings a text contains, the further it moves away from the normal conditions of

---

46 On this subject, see the very precise analysis by Kearns, *Heroes of Attica*, 50–2.

utterance and the more likely it is to stand the test of time and appeal to the greatest number of people. It follows that Sophocles's work has become more literary over the millennia: an utterance that was not originally ambiguous has become so twenty-four centuries later. The author can send his warmest thanks to posterity.

Unless, of course, posterity is mistaken and its definition of literature slightly skewed by the refusal to take into account the contexts of the work. But, in fact, we have no choice when it comes to *Oedipus at Colonus*: the tragedy presents itself to us stripped bare, orphaned of all the places that gave it its coherence. This makes it the ideal literary object, free of any contextual mooring, liable to every interpretation. It is a pure form that marvellously suits the formalists in us: we can applaud gleefully and give free rein to the endless game of commentary.

The trouble is that this pure form is nothing but an artefact of history. *Oedipus at Colonus* is not an Ionic column, perfect in elegance and balance: it is a ruin, a proper ruin, as ruined as the Parthenon is today – except that its state of disrepair is less glaring. Our mistake is merely the product of an optical illusion. When we look at the Winged Victory of Samothrace, we are quite aware that the statue is not complete. If we persist in finding it beautiful despite what is missing or, as André Malraux wrote, specifically *because* of this amputation, and continue to see it as 'the symbol of art',[47] it is with full knowledge of the facts: the reality of this anatomic loss is always present in our mind and can even, if need be, participate in creating the effect of beauty.

Mutatis mutandis, *Oedipus at Colonus* is a Winged Victory of Samothrace, but a Victory we behold under the effect of some mirage that prevents us from realizing it is

---

47 André Malraux, 'La Métamorphose des dieux', in *Écrits sur l'art*, vol. 2 (Œuvres complètes, V) (Paris: Gallimard, 2004), 96 (note).

shorn of both arms and its head. A significant part of *Oedipus at Colonus* got written off by history. To read this play without noticing that, unlike modern literature, it is only delocalized by accident, is to forget everything that makes up the singularity of ancient tragedy. Places, culture, tradition: the elements that cohered in tragedy and were responsible for its meaning and effect have vanished. The failure to realize it is only because this disappearance is fully consonant with our current concept of a delocalized literature. How could we regret the lack of something whose absence fills us with satisfaction?

To understand our pathological relationship with tragedy, we have to imagine a world in which the Winged Victory of Samothrace could be viewed as a faithful, almost banal reproduction of reality, in which no one would admire the genius of an artist and a fate that created it as what we see; a world in which humans have no heads or arms, but do have wings. Yes, it is a grotesque vision, but we hardly have a choice: we have to resort to such images to take notice of our own moral amputation and our indifference to the loss of place in tragedy – this place that today no longer seems to be part of literature, and even appears to belong to its opposite.

In our eyes, literary works are autonomous. Perhaps, but this was not always the case. There have been literatures in which works had an exogenous coherence. Today, *Semimaru*, *Oedipus at Colonus*, Noh drama, and tragedy in general are vestiges of this former state of literature, which reach us as if they had fallen from another planet. It is not that such pieces detached from their context become incomprehensible to us. On the contrary, and here is exactly the problem: we read them all the better, enjoy them all the more, and comment on them all the more freely given that their local aspect has vanished without trace. Despite their best efforts, time has turned them into current literary objects. It has literally done *its* work.

Our admiration is only directed at ruins. Our commentary and our very aesthetic feeling itself are only made possible by the disappearance of place, creating polysemic effects and new ambiguities, putting mystery where once was only obvious fact, and bringing into the world an infinity of contradictory interpretations. Of the place itself, no one can speak: it is unexplainable and even more unexplainable since it has been lost. But this inexplicability forces us to speak *alongside*, opening the field to the game of concepts: delivered from Place, tragedy will become Idea.

First and Second Episodes

Oracles and Liberty

A young woman arrives on horseback, wearing a hat to protect her from the sun. It is Ismene, Oedipus's second daughter. She brings news from Thebes. The civil war is raging. With the backing of his uncle Creon, the younger son Eteocles has chased his older brother Polynices out of his homeland. Polynices is raising an army to recapture the throne. And with new oracles predicting that the city's salvation will depend on Oedipus's tomb, the Thebans are preparing to come and fetch their former king. It is said that Creon will arrive soon.

Oedipus realizes that, due to his crimes, people will only want to bury him at the kingdom's borders. Outraged, he declares that he will refuse to give in to the Thebans' demands and asks Athens for its support, promising the city that he will bring the salvation announced by the oracles.

On the advice of the inhabitants of Colonus, Ismene goes into the sacred woods to offer the Eumenides libations that might win their favour.

At that moment, Creon arrives. He officially grants Oedipus his hospitality and assures him that he will support him against the Thebans. In return, Oedipus confirms that his tomb will become a supernatural rampart for Athens.

2

The Idea

In memoriam Ulrich von Wilamowitz-Moellendorff (1848–1931)

Deprived of place, tragedy is left at the mercy of concepts. We must re-establish its lost coherence. Failing that, how can we explain texts that only functioned in the context of ritual performances and only took on meaning through their geographic location? Theoretical scaffolding serves to hold up works that have escaped their context. But the danger is that we might forget that the scaffolding is not the thing itself, no matter how beautiful or ingenious.

Asked why opium put people to sleep, Molière's trainee doctor answered that it had a sleep-inducing property, whose effect was to dull the senses.[1] To say that was tantamount to saying nothing. One might as well explain the rain by referring to the sky's rainy capacity, or the wind by its windy power.

Many of those who have reflected on tragedy do hardly better than this semi-clever, semi-naïve doctor. For example, the explanation of tragedy through the concept of the tragic. At first glance, how could one possibly disagree? A tragedy is necessarily tragic. That goes without saying. And since we find the tragic all over the place in real life, tragedy quite easily becomes an object with a universal vocation, the

---

1 Molière, *Le Malade imaginaire*, third interlude, in Œuvres complètes (Paris: Gallimard, 'Bibliothèque de la Pléiade', 1971), vol. 2, 1173.

vehicle of a message valid for every era and every country, independent of the particular conditions of its production. This would be the Greek miracle: to have succeeded in inventing forms in which human experience immediately, by a stroke of genius, finds its ideal expression. All we can do is admire its accomplishments.

I will let someone else contest the idea that there was a miracle in Greece. I have spent too much of my life passionately reading Greek literature for such a denial not to ring terribly false, coming from me. I will simply contest the idea that the miracle is situated where so many would place it, and particularly in the concept of the tragic. Or, that if there is a miracle, it might reside in this concept's marvellous capacity to apply a ready-made interpretive blueprint to works, to make apparently intelligible what should never have entered into a framework of intelligibility, and to wrest tragedy from its place of origin. The concept is the enemy of place.

For tragedies have not always been tragic. This may sound surprising, yet it is a proven fact: while there have been tragedies since the sixth century BCE, the tragic has existed for barely two centuries. On the scale of history, it is a very recent invention.

The Tragic According to George W. Bush

What exactly is this invasive *tragic* quality, this opponent that anyone who wants to consider ancient tragedy in an even slightly realistic manner inevitably comes up against? Let's face it, everyone thinks they know what tragedy is. At this point, it is hard to resist sharing a pertinent joke, a fictive – needless to say – but interesting tale, in that it submits several received ideas about tragedy. It is an American story, set during the first term of President George W. Bush, shortly after the terrorist attacks of 11 September 2001:

While visiting an elementary school, President Bush walks into a classroom. The students are in the middle of a vocabulary lesson and the teacher asks the president if he would be willing to lead a discussion of the word 'tragedy'. The illustrious visitor asks the class to give him an example of a tragedy. A little boy stands and offers the following: 'If my best friend who lives next door was hit by a car while he was playing in the street, that would be a tragedy.'

'No,' says the president, 'that would be an accident.'

A little girl raises her hand: 'If a school bus carrying fifty children fell over a cliff and all the passengers were killed, that would be a tragedy.'

'I'm afraid not', explains the president. 'That would be what we call a great loss.'

The class is silent. Now none of the children will dare to suggest an answer. President Bush looks over the classroom: 'Really, none of you can give me a good example of a tragedy?'

Finally, from the very back of the classroom, a little boy raises his hand and calmly speaks up: 'If Air Force One were hit by a missile and reduced to ashes with President and Mrs Bush on board, it would be a tragedy.'

'Excellent!' President Bush exclaims. 'That's exactly it. And can you tell me why it would be a tragedy?'

'Well,' says the boy, 'because it wouldn't be an accident, and it certainly wouldn't be a great loss.'

We should not give this joke more importance than it claims to have. However, it is significant that this attempt to define tragedy never mentions ancient tragedy, despite the fact that, to be absolutely precise, ancient tragedy is the only *real* kind: from a purely historical point of view, the only tragedies are Greek. Any other use of the word, including to refer to the plays of Shakespeare or Racine, only illustrates derivative meanings. Strictly speaking, Racine did not write tragedies, but neo-tragedies. In his vocabulary lesson, George Bush not only never refers to Greek tragedy, but never even brings up theatre: rather than tragedy, it is the tragic that is being addressed, as if the concept had managed completely to overshadow the thing it is supposed to represent (in English, the word 'tragedy' can refer both to the concept and the thing itself, which makes it even easier to confuse the two).

Let us take this joke for what it is, to wit, a digest of clichés about the tragic. From which it appears that, based on the three examples provided (the child hit by a car, the bus accident, the attack on the plane), we call tragic any major misfortune and, particularly, any misfortune involving loss of human life. This is certainly the trivial usage of the term, though we also use it to describe, through hyperbole and in a somewhat diminished sense, events that do not lead to death – such as the bankruptcy of a corporation. However, the joke does not stop at this trivial usage: it offers two important distinctions.

First, a tragedy is not necessarily a 'great loss'. The tragic quality of an event is not linked to the number of victims. The degree of horror and the gravity of a crime are not determining parameters of the definition. A tragedy can be an individual, a familial, or a national misfortune.

Second, a tragedy is not an accident. Here, George Bush touches on an important aspect of the traditional definition of the tragic: an accident is exclusively due to chance, whereas a tragedy would be the effect of intention or of what could more widely be called fate. Philosophically, this is what would distinguish a car crash or a bus accident, even if it involved fifty children, from the destruction of a plane by a missile: an accident is in principle avoidable, while the missile looks for its target – and finds it. The idea of the tragic entails a necessity against which man is powerless. Tragedy therefore has an aspect that is absent from a mere accident, a pure, formless function of chance: it can be interpreted.[2]

From this perspective, *Oedipus at Colonus* is certainly a tragedy in the trivial sense of the term. The succession of events in the play is not governed by chance, but by oracles uttered at the beginning. The first, revealed in the prologue by Oedipus himself, predicts that at the end of his life, after numerous misfortunes, he will take refuge with the Eumenides and become a benefactor to those who welcome him. The second, reported by Ismene, states that Thebes's salvation will depend on its former king, be he dead or alive. The entire series of subsequent episodes specifically results from these two episodes: the arrival of Creon, who has come to get Oedipus, that of Polynices, their respective failures, and Oedipus's death in Athens. None of these events is truly unexpected. They are all contained in germ form in the initial oracles, of which the play seems only to present a fulfilment devoid of surprises.

What is true of *Oedipus at Colonus* is even more true of *Oedipus Rex*. If Oedipus appears as the ultimate tragic figure here, it is not because he combined parricide and incest by killing his father then marrying his mother, thus doubling the monstrosity of his first crime. The number of unfortunate events has no bearing on the issue: it does not change the nature of these evils nor does it mechanically turn them into tragedy. Oedipus's life is only tragic, in the trivial sense of the term, because this parricide and this incest are the signs of a divine conspiracy: they fulfil a fate that had been announced by an oracle even before Oedipus's birth – a fate that comes from beyond the perceptible world, which foils the will and precautions of mortal, reasonable beings.

---

2 Curiously, the distinction between tragedy and the accident was discussed by Raymond Williams in terms very similar to those found in the joke about George W. Bush: 'I once heard it said that if "you or I" went out and got run over by a bus, that would not be tragedy.' *Modern Tragedy* [1966] (Peterborough: Broadview, 2001), 48.

Neither Oedipus's parents nor Oedipus himself, having been warned about this oracle, can change anything about it. This is the essence of transcendence: it is beyond the realities here on earth; it cannot be measured on their scale.

Many modern tragedies follow the tragic model suggested by President Bush. Young Hamlet, prince of Denmark, seeks to avenge the death of the king, his murdered father, and fails in his attempt. Fate manifests itself here in the fact that the task of revenge has been assigned to Hamlet by the ghost of the king himself, appearing at the beginning of the play. The prince rushes towards his own destruction through the effect of a supernatural injunction, which marks the intervention of transcendence.

But it is not necessary for this transcendence to manifest as a truly supernatural form of the beyond. Even in *Hamlet*, the paternal apparition can be seen as a metaphor for the filial duty of revenge. The transcendence belongs to the realm of moral law. In the final analysis, the ghost could simply be an internal demand on the part of the character of Hamlet, the result of a mere hallucination, without changing anything about this story's tragic nature. A *Hamlet* without a ghost would still be a tragedy.

Passion or madness can play the role of transcendence. Both were considered by the Greeks to be sacred afflictions, sent by the gods, inexorably imposing themselves upon individuals. This is the case with Phaedra's shameful passion for her son-in-law Hippolytus. A version of *Phaedra* shorn of mythology or the supernatural would yield a perfectly acceptable tragedy, in which any transcendence would be of a purely psychological nature.

The same is true for the family, the clan and the nation: the social group functions as a tragic agent so long as it introduces the transcendence of a pressing ideal in individuals' consciousness. In the name of Rome, the warrior Horace sacrifices those who are closest to him. There is nothing supernatural here:

the transcendence is of a political and social nature. Similarly, in *Romeo and Juliet*, the two protagonists' families and clans play the part of a transcendent tragic force, without any intervention from a supernatural power. Yet this remains a tragedy, in the sense proposed by President Bush.

Should we be surprised that a jest devoid of the least conceptual ambition can explain some of the greatest masterpieces of the stage? That would be giving a lot of credit to a mere wisecrack – or to the genius of an American president. The definition of the tragic sketched here is essentially only that of its commonly accepted sense, and if the latter can apparently be applied in a more or less correct way (which is not always the case with the commonly accepted), this is because it is itself the heir to an entire philosophical tradition of examination of tragedy. But – to repeat – this is a very recent tradition. It has existed for barely over two centuries, while tragedy was invented in Greece more than two and a half millennia ago. This discrepancy certainly raises a few questions.

The Aristotelian Beginnings of the Tragic

While the word *tragic* (*tragikos*) does exist in ancient Greek, it was initially only an adjective, referring to everything related to the genre of tragedy. One can speak of a tragic chorus or tragic poetry, but a tragedy is itself no more tragic than the psyche is psychic or water is aquatic.

However, what is *related* to tragedy can quite easily pass for what *specifically belongs* to it. This shift in meaning first appeared in Aristotle. Which is hardly surprising, given that the philosopher sought to discern the 'essence'[3] (*ousia*) of his

---

3 Aristotle, *Poetics*, VI, 1449 b 24. [Translator's note: Ferguson translates *ousia* as 'formal definition', but 'essence' is more appropriate in this context.]

subject, in other words to provide it with a non-situated definition. Had he been less interested in tragedy's essence than in its existence, he might have defined it as the type of performance staged in Athens on certain occasions, during certain religious festivals (the Lenaia and the City Dionysia), with certain specific staging and musical requirements. This definition could have satisfied the most rigorous criteria possible and prevented the confusion between tragedy and any other kind of performance. However, this was not the goal that Aristotle set himself: the practical circumstances of the tragic performance mattered little to him.

The philosopher's lack of interest in the actual reality of the performance is a recurring source of disappointment to the contemporary reader of the *Poetics*. Aristotle's relative indifference to tragedy as a performance is accentuated by the fact that his relationship to traditional tragic ritual was extremely distant. Not an Athenian by birth, he arrived in the Attic city some forty years after the end of the golden age of tragedy, at a time when performance conditions had significantly changed. His knowledge of tragedy was partially drawn from books.[4]

In practice, Aristotle uses the adjective *tragikos* to contrast, for example, the mode of imitation (*mimesis*) with the epic.[5] An obvious opposition, in so far as tragedy involves actors while in the epic the poet is the only one to speak. In this case, the adjective 'tragic' does not involve any a priori definition of tragedy. It refers to a characteristic and manifest feature of the tragic performance.

But things are already a little different on the occasions when Aristotle distinguishes between the 'most tragic' tragedies and those that are apparently less tragic.[6] To draw this

4   See Florence Dupont, *Aristote ou le vampire du théâtre occidental* (Paris: Flammarion, 2007), 32–4.
5   Aristotle, *Poetics*, ch. XXVI, 1461 b 1.
6   Ibid., ch. XIII, 1452 b 37; 1453 a 27–30.

distinction is to create within the empirical corpus of all tragedies a partition, not to say a hierarchy, based on a definition of the object of tragedy that is deductive, rather than inductive as before; it is to speak not of what tragedy is, but of what it should be, replacing the objective examination of reality with a theoretical reflection on ideas and essences, and, if need be, accusing reality of not living up to the model to which we would like it to conform. With Aristotle, the concept makes its first appearance in the long history of the reception of Greek tragedy. It will never quite leave it, and its aura will sometimes eclipse even the empirical existence of tragedy.

The Philosophical Tragic

It is a long way from Aristotle to the tragic according to George Bush, however. Strange as it may seem, the question had never been approached from this angle until 1795, when Schelling proposed a reflection on the philosophical meaning of Greek tragedy. No one had ever thought to define the tragic (*das Tragische*, *die Tragik*) as the conflict between man and fate – a definition familiar to any fool today. But the commonplace had simply not yet been found.

Just a few years earlier, in 1792, Schiller had already suggested a moral interpretation of tragedy in a meditation on 'the cause of the pleasure we derive from tragic objects'. But Schiller was still trying to resolve the old Aristotelian problem of the paradoxical pleasure specific to tragedy: how can one delight in the staged representation of the pain of others? He answered by showing that this pleasure was of a moral order and that 'the highest moral pleasure is always accompanied by pain':

[The realm of tragedy] embraces all the possible cases in which any purpose of nature is sacrificed to a moral purpose,

49

or a moral purpose is sacrificed to that purpose of nature, which is higher.[7]

As concerned as he is by the drama's ethical dimension, Schiller does not raise questions that stray beyond the aesthetic and artistic context: as a theatre practitioner, he was merely trying to write the best tragedy possible. In that respect, he was no longer interested in Greek tragedy as such: in his view, modern tragedies such as the plays of Shakespeare and Corneille, as well as his own works, seemed far better suited to the tragic ideal.[8] In his conceptual treatment of ancient tragedy, the form only appears as the imperfect and historically limited realization of an eternal essence, and the theoretical tragedy nearly eclipses the empirical tragedy.

Schelling took another step towards the derealization of tragedy. The question he raises is no longer principally aesthetic; it is no longer a matter of thinking about tragedy's effects on the audience, the way Schiller did. All that interests him is the metaphysical question of freedom, of which he finds the best illustration in Greek tragedy:

[It] honoured human freedom by making its hero *fight* against the superior power of fate. In order not to go beyond the limits of art, the tragedy had to let him succumb. Nevertheless, in order to make restitution for this humiliation of human freedom extorted by art, it had to let him *atone* even for the crime committed by *fate*. As long as he is still free, he holds out against the power of destiny. As soon as he succumbs he ceases to be free. Succumbing, he still accuses fate for the loss of his freedom.[9]

---

7 Friedrich Schiller, *Über den Grund des Vergnügens an tragischen Gegenständen* [On the cause of the pleasure we derive from tragic objects, 1792], in *Werke*, vol. 20, part 1 (Weimar: Böhlaus, 1962), 138.

8 Friedrich Schiller, *Über die tragische Kunst* [On the tragic art, 1792], in *Werke*, vol. 20, part 1 (Weimar: Böhlaus, 1962), 155–6.

9 Friedrich Wilhelm Joseph von Schelling, *Philosophical Letters on*

At the lofty heights of abstraction and generalization reached by Schelling's thinking, no play is referred to by name: philosophical speculation can only proceed at the cost of this silence. But it is clear that the implicit model here is *Oedipus Rex*, in which the hero, guilty despite himself, freely accepts the punishment for the crimes that fate made him commit.

The path is not so long from this masterful reading of Greek tragedy to the particularly trivial version in our satirical tale about George W. Bush: the same speculative chain stretches from one end to the other. It also includes the *Course of Lectures on Dramatic Art and Literature* delivered in Vienna in 1808 by Schlegel, formulations from which would become a kind of dogma throughout Europe:

> Inward liberty and external necessity are the two poles of the tragic world. Each of these ideas can only appear in the most perfect manner by contrast with the other.
>
> The ennobled painting of man and that of his struggle with fate is the essence of the tragic in the sense of the ancients.[10]

Then come the *Aesthetics*, the lectures on fine art Hegel delivered beginning in 1820, in which he tried to develop an essentially dialectical concept of tragedy, putting a more sophisticated spin on Schlegel's double definition. According to Hegel, the ultimate tragic conflict is not that between man and fate, but the conflict between two equivalent moral bodies:

Dogmatism and Criticism (*Philosophische Briefe über Dogmatismus und Kritizismus*, 1795), 10th letter, in *The Unconditional in Human Knowledge: Four Early Essays*, 1794–1796, trans. Fritz Marti (Lewisburg, PA: Bucknell University Press, 1980), 192–3.

10 August Wilhelm von Schlegel, *Course of Lectures on Dramatic Art and Literature* (*Vorlesungen über dramatische Kunst und Literatur*, 1809–1811), trans. John Black (London: Baldwin, Cradock and Joy, 1815), 73, 74. John Black's translation has been updated here. On the dissemination of the ideas of the first wave of German Romanticism, see Bernard Franco, *Le Despotisme du goût: Débats sur le modèle tragique allemand en France, 1797–1814* (Göttingen: Wallstein, 2006), 2 vols.

The original essence of tragedy consists then in the fact that within such a conflict each of the opposed sides, if taken by itself, has *justification*; while each can establish the true and positive content of its own aim and character only by denying and infringing the equally justified power of the other. The consequence is that in its moral life, and because of it, each is nevertheless involved in *guilt*.[11]

The model here is less *Oedipus Rex* than *Antigone*: Creon embodies reason of state versus Antigone, who represents familial devotion. According to Hegel, this tragic conflict is only apparent. It implicitly points to a transcendent harmony that cannot be realized on earth:

Above mere fear and tragic sympathy there therefore stands that sense of reconciliation which the tragedy affords by the glimpse of eternal justice. In its absolute sway this justice overrides the relative justification of one-sided aims and passions because it cannot suffer the conflict and contradiction of naturally harmonious ethical powers to be victorious and permanent in truth and actuality.[12]

Tragic theatre therefore teaches the absolute character of the moral norm. If there is a tomb of Oedipus to be found anywhere, it is here, in this refusal to consider the Greek tragedies as anything other than the almost superfluous illustration of a system of concepts: Oedipus truly dies when his body is taken away from us, when place totally disappears and is replaced by the triumph of the most abstract and general idea. Another Romantic philosopher, Solger,

11 Georg Wilhelm Friedrich Hegel, *Aesthetics: Lectures on Fine Art* (*Vorlesungen über die Ästhetik*, posthumous, 1835), trans. T. M. Knox (Oxford: Clarendon Press, 1975), vol. 2, 1196 (3rd part, s. III, ch. III, III, C, 3, a–523).
12 Ibid., 1198 (526).

found his own way to express much the same thing in the
1810s:

> The essential element of dramatic art does not rest on
> particular subjects and points of view, but on its capacity to
> grasp the intimate essence of every human action and life, the
> Idea ... The tragic principle is when all reality, as the pres-
> entation and revelation of the idea, appears contradicting
> itself and immersing itself in the idea.[13]

If such a submission of reality to the Idea is the basis of 'the
tragic principle' according to Solger, it ironically also constitutes the very principle of explanation by the tragic:
replacing the reality of tragedy by the idea of which it is
supposed to be the historical embodiment. The shift from
tragedy to the tragic offers no more than a derealization of
ancient tragedy in favour of concepts from German Romanticism, a process to which Schiller, Schelling, Hegel and
Solger contributed, as we have seen, along with Hölderlin,
Goethe, Schopenhauer, and Vischer, among many others.[14]
Here, the text of the play is treated solely as a pretext for
philosophical discourse. It loses all its substance: the actors
drop their masks and robes and leave the stage, soon followed by the chorus and the musicians; the stage wraps itself
in clouds; its outlines blur and gradually disappear into
space; eventually, instead of a theatre, there is nothing left
but a great void, the mere memory of a dream, fit to be filled
by concepts.

---

13 Karl Wilhelm Ferdinand Solger, *Vorlesungen über Ästhetik*
[Lessons on aesthetics], ed. K. W. L. Heyse (Leipzig: Brockhaus,
posthumous, 1829), 309; partially cited by Peter Szondi, *An Essay on the
Tragic*, trans. Paul Fleming (Stanford, CA: Stanford University Press,
2002), 23.
14 See Szondi's masterful essay, ibid.

The False Nietzschean Rupture

Nietzsche was one of the first to protest against the excessive conceptualization of ancient tragedy in his time. Admittedly, the author of *The Birth of Tragedy* in many respects fitted right in with the long tradition of thinkers of the tragic, notably through the influence of Schopenhauer on his own work. However, unlike his predecessors, he sought to return to the historical reality of the plays and the material circumstances of their performance. Putting the stage back at the centre of his thinking, he adopted the spectator's point of view and dismissed three of the most famous theories about tragedy: those that seek to characterize 'the struggle of the hero with fate, the triumph of the moral world order, or the purgation of the emotions through tragedy, as the essence of the tragic'.[15] The triple allusion is clear: Schlegel and Schelling are the first targets, then Schiller and Hegel, and finally Aristotle. Each represents the failure of a line of thought that misunderstands tragedy's own nature and subordinates it to moral, social, or psychological utility.

According to Nietzsche, one must no longer *interpret* tragedy, or in other words attempt to give it a meaning, whatever that is. Instead, one must first feel it in one's flesh, like a contemporary spectator of Aeschylus, Sophocles or Euripides. An impossible undertaking, of course. So Nietzsche turns for help to two things less contradictory than complementary. On the one hand, philology, which allows one to get as close as possible to the historical reality of tragedy. Against the philosophical method of apprehending reality through concepts, *The Birth of Tragedy* asserts that it is necessary to

---

15 Friedrich Nietzsche, *The Birth of Tragedy* (*Die Geburt der Tragödie*, 1872), trans. Walter Kaufmann (New York: Random House, 1967), 132 (s. 22).

grasp reality prior to any subsequent conceptualization. The philosopher is replaced by the philologist.

But philology is not enough: it fails to get back to reality. In this particular case, this fundamental impossibility is aggravated by our scant sources of information about tragedy. The philological grasp must therefore be completed by an analogical detour, by which one identifies in contemporary experience, accessible to all, a reality liable to shed light on ancient tragedy. In the previous chapter, we found this reality was Noh drama; for Nietzsche, it was Wagnerian opera. Philology describes tragedy from the outside, grasping it in an ever tighter network of erudite references; the analogy, or the detour through the contemporary and through the ordinary apprehension of the world, provides the illusion of tasting the thing itself.

Knowledge and experience, the objective and the subjective: this is the alliance required to reach a complete understanding of tragedy. According to Nietzsche, this is also the actual mechanism of tragedy: the confrontation of Apollo and Dionysus, of appearance and existence, of the objective and the subjective, or, to put it in Schopenhauerian terms, of representation and will,[16] is the driving force of Greek tragedy. In the same way that Hegel claimed tragedy was as dialectical as the Hegelian method and that Solger's explanation of tragedy followed the same lines as the tragic principle (the subordination of reality to the Idea), *The Birth of Tragedy* proposes to describe tragedy by laying claim to the tragic mechanism itself. This empathic attraction of the discourse to its object reveals both the ambition and the limitations of the project; Nietzsche would reproach himself for this in his strikingly lucid 'Attempt at Self-Criticism', published in 1886, fourteen years after the book's first edition.

---

16 On Nietzsche's transposition of Schopenhauer's metaphysical concepts into aesthetic terms, see Szondi, *An Essay on the Tragic*, 41–2.

There is ultimately more continuity from Hegel and Solger to Nietzsche than *The Birth of Tragedy* cares to admit: the rupture is more strongly expressed in the principles proclaimed and the general method than in the results. Admittedly, Nietzsche appears to move away from the frenzied conceptualization to which tragedy was subjected before him: he returns to the historical reality of its performances, in so far as philology allows him to reconstruct it, and emphasizes the fundamental importance of music in the tragic experience. In fact, music is ostensibly neither Schellingian fate, nor Hegelian moral law, nor the Solgerian Idea: it is a perceptible reality that is not immediately reducible to any concept. According to a definition Nietzsche borrowed from Schopenhauer, it is even prior to every concept.[17]

The problem is that we know very little about music in Attic tragedy. We know that a large part of the performance was sung, accompanied by flute and percussion; we surmise that the chorus performed in rhythm; we are aware that Aeschylus, Sophocles and Euripides were as much composers as playwrights. But only tiny fragments remain of ancient scores, and even these are difficult to interpret. Based on that, it is hard to evaluate music's specific role in the tragic system. It is even more perilous to see it as the key that would open the arcana of tragedy to us: one might as well try to build a house out of wind. Lacking Greek music, Nietzsche takes Wagner as a reference, despite the fact that the German composer's music would be far removed from that of Greek tragedy, if only because it makes powerful use of the resources of harmony, something totally unknown to ancient musicians.

---

17 See Nietzsche, *Birth of Tragedy*, 100 (ch. XVI); Arthur Schopenhauer, *Die Welt als Wille und Vorstellung* [The world as will and representation], 1819, III, ch. LII.

But music itself was but a pretext: the philosopher-philologist soon likens all its power and effects to those of the 'dissonance' of which Wagner adroitly makes use in many of his most dramatic set pieces, such as the death of Isolde. Behind dissonance, one does not have to look very far to recognize, barely concealed, some of the favourite concepts of Romantic reflection on the tragic, derived from Kantian antinomies: the conflict between man and the universe, the split of the individual between will and representation, and the tension between subject and object, freedom and nature, and unconditioned and conditioned.[18] In the final analysis, Nietzsche only admires tragedy because it so marvellously illustrates his own idea of the world. Dissonance is the concept he substitutes for the actual reality of these plays: once again, we are faced with the triumph of the idea; once again, tragedy has taken a back seat to the tragic.

The Incoherence of the Tragic

Despite his claims, Nietzsche did not put an end to the long history of the tragic. It continued after him, at least up to Unamuno, who Christianized the concept, and on to the pre-Marxist Lukács, whose analyses of tragedy remain steeped in Hegelianism, and to George Steiner, who sees tragedy as a vast corpus including, without too much strain, Aeschylus and Sophocles as well as Shakespeare and Racine.[19] And the notion of the tragic remains alive and well

18 See Pierre Judet de La Combe, *Les tragédies grecques sont-elles tragiques? Théâtre et théorie* (Paris: Bayard, 2010), 178.

19 Miguel de Unamuno, *The Tragic Sense of Life in Men and Nations* (*Del sentimiento trágico de la vida en los hombres y en los pueblos*, 1913), trans. Anthony Kerrigan (Princeton, NJ: Princeton University Press, 1972). György Lukács, 'The Metaphysics of Tragedy: Paul Ernst', in *Soul and Form* (*Die Seele und die Formen*, 1911), trans. Anna Bostock (New York: Columbia University Press, 2010), 175–98; *The Theory of the Novel* (*Die*

to this day, both in the common understanding and also in literary studies, with little sign that successive challenges to it have had much influence. Alas, the forces of inertia prevail. Yet plenty of warnings were sounded. Walter Benjamin's warning was one of the strongest, because it came from a philosopher of that particular German tradition so central to the history of the tragic. In 1928, his thesis *The Origin of German Tragic Drama* refuted the idea of a permanence of tragedy in the modern era and opposed the philosophical concept of a tragic sense that could be recognized as identical in various forms of theatre, through various eras, and even in everyday life.[20] If there is no tragic discernible here and there, how can tragedy retain the trans-historical dimension we so smugly attribute to it? According to Benjamin, Greek tragedy can only be understood in its historical context, like a sacrifice accomplished in the context of a competition. He goes on to deliver the most factual and objective definition of Greek tragedy possible, quoting from the greatest Hellenist of his time, Ulrich von Wilamowitz-Moellendorff, with whom Nietzsche had violently clashed after the publication of his *Birth of Tragedy*:

An Attic tragedy is a self-contained piece of heroic legend, poetically adapted in the sublime style for presentation by a chorus of Attic citizens and two or three actors, and intended for performance as part of the public worship at the shrine of Dionysus.[21]

Theorie des Romans, 1920), trans. Anna Bostock (Cambridge, MA: MIT Press, 1971), 40–6. George Steiner, *The Death of Tragedy* (London: Faber and Faber, 1961).

20 Walter Benjamin, *The Origin of German Tragic Drama* (*Ursprung des deutschen Trauerspiels*, 1928), trans. John Osborne (London: New Left Books, 1977), 102–20. Rejected by the University of Frankfurt, this thesis was never defended.

21 Ulrich von Wilamowitz-Moellendorff, *What Is an Attic Tragedy? Introduction to Greek Tragedy* [1889], trans. Lisanna Calvi and Stefan

After all the speculation of the German idealist tradition, one could hardly come back down to earth with a more resounding thump. Recess is over. As early as 1889, Wilamowitz was raising every alarm: no, Greek tragedy is not a universal paradigm; it is 'not necessary for [it] to end "tragically" nor to be "tragic"' and it does not even bring into play the celebrated 'fate' (*Schicksal*) that people have so often wanted to see in it.[22] Philology must finally reassert its rights over this object. Tragedy must be wrested from the tragic and the idea.

So, are Greek tragedies tragic? That is the question.[23] Some tragedies undeniably are: *Antigone* and *Oedipus Rex*, for instance. But the tragic in *Oedipus Rex* has little in common with the tragic in *Antigone*, as we have noted: one corresponds to the Schellingian definition of the concept (the hero's struggle against necessity), the other to the one provided by Hegel (the apparent collision of two moral imperatives). Hegel himself turns Schelling's tragic into a mere dialectical moment in the development of the concept, which is acknowledgement enough that these two definitions of the tragic are not identical. Is it really a surprise, then, that the theory of the tragic can successfully be applied to certain plays in the Greek corpus, given that the definition was specifically drawn from those few plays and, further, that it changes from one play to another? Only if it is reckoned a surprise to arbitrarily remove a piece from a puzzle, return it to its initial spot a few seconds later, and discover

---

Rabanus (Verona: *Skenè. Journal of Theatre and Drama Studies*, 2016), 199 (*Einleitung in die griechische Tragödie* [Berlin: Weidmann, 1907], 107); quoted by Benjamin, *Origin of German Tragic Drama*, 106. On the quarrel between Nietzsche and Wilamowitz, see William Marx, *Vie du lettré* (Paris: Minuit, 2009), 129–37.

22 Wilamowitz-Moellendorff, *What Is an Attic Tragedy?*, 41, 211 and 219, respectively (*Einleitung in die griechische Tragödie*, 43–4, 112, 118).

23 This question is borrowed from Judet de La Combe's remarkable essay, *Les tragédies grecques sont-elles tragiques?* though the answer given here is a little different.

that it fits perfectly. It would be more surprising if the puzzle piece fitted equally well in other places, but that never happens. Or, when it does fit elsewhere, it is because we have deliberately recut the piece ad hoc. But, of course, what we are then holding is no longer the same piece of the puzzle.

The tragic functions in the same way. It is an eminently accommodating concept: for some, it only applies to Aeschylus and Sophocles, excluding Euripides; for others, its history continues until the seventeenth century, but sadly no later; for yet others, on the contrary, it is at its peak precisely in the modern era; and finally, for the majority, it almost indifferently covers all of dramatic production from Antiquity to the present day, from Aeschylus to Chekhov, Strindberg and Beckett, and this merry hodgepodge also extends to everyday life.[24]

Portrait of Labiche as a Great Tragic Author

How do you find your way through such a cacophony? Let us have a bit of fun and accept that there are tragic Greek tragedies, in the philosophical sense of the term. But are they any more tragic than other plays that have nothing to do

---

24 In these four distinctive points of view on the tragic, the reader will have recognized, respectively, those of Nietzsche, Steiner, Schiller, and Raymond Williams. In the last category, a few more recent titles can be cited: Jean-Marie Domenach, *Le Retour du tragique* (Paris: Seuil, 1973); Ion Omesco, *La Métamorphose de la tragédie* (Paris: Presses Universitaires de France, 1978); Bennett Simon, *Tragic Drama and the Family: Psychoanalytical Studies from Aeschylus to Beckett* (New Haven, CT: Yale University Press, 1988); Brenda J. Powell, *The Metaphysical Quality of the Tragic: A Study of Sophocles, Giraudoux, and Sartre* (New York: Peter Lang, 1990); William Storm, *After Dionysus: A Theory of the Tragic* (Ithaca, NY: Cornell University Press, 1998); Felicity Rosslyn, *Tragic Plots: A New Reading from Aeschylus to Lorca* (Aldershot: Ashgate, 2000); Paul Vanden Berghe, Christian Biet and Karel Vanhaesebrouck, eds, *Œdipe contemporain? Tragédie, tragique, politique* (Vic la Gardiole: L'Entretemps, 2007). Note that C. Biet takes a far more critical position on the concept of the tragic in *La Tragédie* (Paris: Armand Colin, 1997), 171–7.

with tragedy, or Greece? Are they more tragic than a good nineteenth-century French vaudeville like *The Italian Straw Hat*, for example? The play's plot is well known: Fadinard's horse eats a hat hanging from a tree; forced to replace it, Fadinard heads out in search of a similar hat, dragging after him in his mad dash the entire wedding party assembled to celebrate his nuptials. A transgression committed unintentionally, through the work of fate; a responsibility freely accepted; an expiation assented to with no less freedom; a hero struggling against necessity: are not these all the ingredients of the tragic according to Schelling?

Claude Lévi-Strauss was the first brilliantly to demonstrate that the plot of *The Italian Straw Hat* follows the same structural plan as *Oedipus Rex*. While searching for a murderer, Oedipus learns that he is himself guilty of the crime; while searching for a hat identical to the lost one, Fadinard discovers that 'the hat they have been looking for is none other than the hat that was destroyed'.[25] Let us put the finishing touch to Lévi-Strauss's demonstration: not only do the two plays share the same structure, but *Oedipus Rex* is no more tragic than Eugène Labiche's work.

And, if *The Italian Straw Hat* is Labiche's *Oedipus Rex*, *Mr Perrichon's Holiday* would be his *Antigone*. This comedy's dramatic device could not be simpler: the generosity and helpfulness of Armand Desroches, suitor to Mr Perrichon's daughter Henriette, seriously upset her father, who would prefer to give her hand to another suitor, Daniel Savary, whose life he believes he has saved. 'You owe me everything, everything!' Perrichon says to Daniel, before 'nobly' adding: 'I shall never forget it!'[26] Perrichon is the seat of a conflict

25 Claude Lévi-Strauss, *The Jealous Potter* (*La Potière jalouse*, Paris: Plon, 1985), trans. Benedicte Chorier (Chicago: University of Chicago Press, 1988), 199.

26 Eugène Labiche, *Le Voyage de monsieur Perrichon* (II, X), in *Théâtre*, vol. 2 (Paris: Bordas, 'Classiques Garnier', 1991), 481.

between the social obligation of gratitude, which places him in debt to Armand, and the concern for freedom and moral autonomy, which paradoxically prompts him to favour the man to whom he owes nothing. Social duty will finally prevail, much in the way that reason of state, embodied by Creon in *Antigone*, overrides familial devotion as represented by his niece. In other words, *Mr Perrichon's Holiday* is Labiche's most Hegelian tragedy, in that it presents the conflict between two apparently contradictory moral authorities that are ultimately reconciled when Perrichon understands that his freedom and dignity are not incompatible with the expression of the gratitude he owes to Armand. After Schelling and *The Italian Straw Hat*, Hegel makes his grand entrance on the vaudeville stage.

Let us go a little further: could we not say that these plays feature the tragic irony so emphatically celebrated by Solger, and at a far more acute level than in the Attic tragedies? The constant asides to the audience, the comic distance, the characters torn between their free will and the awareness of being playthings of their passions and of events: all of this lifts the irony in both these works to heights perhaps unknown to the Ancients. It is tempting to take that extra step and declare these vaudevilles to be at least as tragic, if not more so, than the ancient tragedies.

The Problem of Happy Tragedies

One might object that there is a fundamental difference separating such comedies from Greek tragedies: the absence of death. The conflict Labiche's characters encounter never put them at mortal risk. The moral struggle is never paid for with a life, contrary to Schelling's thesis, which requires that the tragic hero ultimately succumb, a victim of fate.

How does one reply to that? First of all, obviously, by noting that the classification of vaudevilles as tragic works is to be taken *cum grano salis*: we do so primarily to call into question the soundness of the concept of the tragic and the preconceptions that go with it. However, let us defend the hypothesis to the end and, rather than wriggle out of it, take the game seriously. First, the observation that forms the basis of the objection is not accurate: contrary to what is claimed, Labiche's plays do feature mortal perils, if not actual deaths. Monsieur Perrichon narrowly escapes a duel that would have cost him his life, and later nearly falls into a chasm. The same happens to Daniel Savary – apparently, at least.

To be generous, let us admit that these perils are never very great and, most importantly, never what is essentially at stake in the conflict. But does that force us to accept the objection that contrasts tragic heroes meeting dreadful fates with vaudeville characters living comfy lives? It would, if ancient tragedies were indeed littered with dead bodies or at least all ended with the hero's death. Yet this is not the case. And we can even push a little further: not only do most tragedies not end with the hero's death, but the majority do not even end unhappily. That is certainly one of the strongest objections one can raise to the theory of the tragic. One of the most provocative, too, in terms of what is commonly accepted.

So, ancient tragedies do not have unhappy endings? What about *Antigone*, *Oedipus Rex*, *Medea*? Clearly, these dramas do not end in joy and merriment. But the argument is not conclusive, for one could easily name other plays that may not necessarily have an absolutely happy ending, but certainly finish more happily than they began: *Oedipus at Colonus*, *Orestes* and *Philoctetes*, for example. And there are also tragedies whose denouement is resolutely happy: one might mention, among others, *Ion* and *Iphigenia in Tauris*. Some have even seen Euripides's *Helen* as a comedy or, at the least, a parody, though that assessment may be somewhat over the top.[27] Be that as it may, *Helen* is certainly no less comic, *mutatis mutandis*, than *Mr Perrichon's Holiday* is tragic. All things considered, if Labiche created a tragedy in a vaudeville, who is to say that Euripides did not try his hand at parody in a tragedy?

The hypothesis is all the more plausible given that Euripides, like Aeschylus and Sophocles, did indeed write and stage comedies and farces, for these are the dramatic forms that most closely resemble the satyr play that concluded any Athenian trilogy of tragedies. We too often forget that a quarter of the works of the great Greek tragedians consisted of farcical plays, of which a regrettably small number have reached us. Additionally, the difference between a tragedy and a satyr play was not so great: sometimes a tragedy served as the last part of a tetralogy, rather than the usual satyr play. This is what Euripides did with *Alcestis*.

Contrary to what the words would have us believe, not every tragedy is tragic, in the philosophical sense of the term. This problem was set out by Aristotle himself. The philosopher noted that a tragedy can equally describe 'a change from bad fortune to good, or from good fortune to bad'.[28] To be sure, he considered Euripides's 'most tragic' (*tragikôtatai*) works those which 'end unhappily'[29] – a judgement that clearly demonstrates Aristotle's constant search for the essence of tragedy. But it is a long way from this Aristotelian essence of tragedy to the idea of the tragic championed by German idealist philosophy. The Greek philosopher does not set the unhappy ending as a condition of tragedy; it is a mere parameter reinforcing the play's dramatic effectiveness. As

---

27 See Arthur Woollgar Verrall, *Essays on Four Plays of Euripides: Andromache, Helen, Heracles, Orestes* (Cambridge: Cambridge University Press, 1905), 50 sqq.; cited (and contested) by Henri Grégoire in his 1950 French edition of Euripides, *Hélène* (Paris: Belles Lettres, 1985), 37–9.

28 Aristotle, *Poetics*, ch. VII, 1451 a 13–14.

29 Ibid., ch. XIII, 1453 a 23–30.

we saw above, Aristotle never regarded the tragic as a concept defined a priori, with clearly delimited contours: it was more like a scale against which to measure the reality of tragedy according to a subtle gradation.

Yet the author of the *Poetics* is explicitly opposed to 'those who censure Euripides' for giving his tragedies an unhappy ending. This suggests that there was debate on the matter, and that the opinion contrary to Aristotle's may well have been that of the majority: people sometimes preferred tragedies with happy endings. The tragic as it would be defined by Schelling, with the hero crushed by fate, had not yet appeared. Furthermore, it is only relatively recently that the tragic has been exclusively identified with a story that ends badly and that the adjective has become a synonym of 'fateful' in everyday language. In the seventeenth century, Corneille could still refer to the 'happy tragedy'[30] as opposed to the tragedy with an unhappy ending, allowing to both their rightful place. At the time, the Italians considered *tragedia a lieto fine* a genre as legitimate as any other.

Faced with this ultimately unavoidable reality, Hegel and Nietzsche have no choice but to accommodate these happy plays within their systems, defined as tragedies of reconciliation, in which the moral powers previously in conflict are able to come to an agreement and find peace.[31] But, according to both philosophers, the character of such works is exceptional and their existence tends to manifest the dialectical takeover, or even decadence of tragedy, of the only real tragedy: the sort with a fateful ending.

---

30 Pierre Corneille, *Discours de l'utilité et des parties du poème dramatique* [Discourse on the utility and parts of dramatic poetry, 1660], in Œuvres complètes, ed. André Stegmann (Paris: Seuil, 1963), 824.

31 See Hegel, *Aesthetics*, vol. 3, 1218–19 (3rd part, s. III, ch. III, III, C, 3, c–551); Nietzsche, *Birth of Tragedy*, 109 (ch. 17).

The Hermeneutical Circle of the Tragic

The tradition of the happy tragedy was gradually swept aside by the German Romantics and their epigones, to the point that even its memory has now vanished, including among the most authoritative Hellenists. For instance, here speaks one of the most knowledgeable scholars on Euripides:

> Ancient tragedy offers the sight of men's fight against fate and the gods, an uneven fight that most often ends in suffering and death, but that exalts human dignity.[32]

Very well: if this definition is intended as a digest of Schelling's thought, we can only approve. But if it happens to be an attempt to describe Greek tragedy, stop right there! After the strong but enlightened warnings of Wilamowitz-Moellendorff, the philosophical refutation delivered by Benjamin, and abundant criticism of the reckless application of the modern concept of the tragic to Attic tragedy,[33] how can some of the best-informed philologists continue to be taken in by such a chimera? Are we eternally doomed to see Athenian tragedy through the prism of a concept of the world primarily devised in the little city of Jena, in the duchy of Saxe-Weimar, in Germany, on the cusp of the nineteenth century? Not that this Romantic concept of the tragic lacks interest in and of itself. On the contrary, it is one of the most remarkable objects of thought to have emerged in the last centuries of the history of philosophy, a pure product of German idealism's critique of Kantianism. The concept's lasting prominence testifies to its exceptional richness and

---

32 François Jouan, in his edition of *Rhésos* (*Rhesus*), attributed to Euripides (Paris: Belles Lettres, 2004), LV.

33 Among French scholars, most notably in the works of Florence Dupont, Nicole Loraux, Jean-Pierre Vernant and Pierre Vidal-Naquet.

versatility: one could almost regret such a polyvalence.[34] But it is high time we freed ourselves of this ideology when considering the ancient texts – or, at least, invoked it more shrewdly.

Why is this so difficult? The answer to that question might allow us to lance the boil, so to speak. The main difficulty resides in the fact that the idea of the tragic undeniably applies quite nicely to the tragedies that are best known and most admired today, considered models of their type. But are they models of their type because they satisfy the concept of the tragic? Or was the concept only created to explain this handful of masterpieces? When it comes to tragedy, aesthetic assessment is inextricably combined with philosophical conceptualization, and it is well nigh impossible to know which came first.

The Problem with Euripides

To escape the hermeneutical circle and travel back into the genealogy of the idea of the tragic, it is important to acknowledge that the various concepts of the tragic developed over time function very well with a few tragedies, moderately with many, and poorly or not at all with a significant number of them. Such heterogeneity constantly raises problems and demands a deeper look into the specifics. Sophocles and Aeschylus basically pass the test, though with major disparities. If *Oedipus Rex* and *Antigone* present themselves as tragic plays par excellence (anything less would have been surprising, given they were the basis for the development of the concept), Sophocles's other works do not so brilliantly

---

34 Betokening the concept's currency, 'the tragic' was the theme of the Salzburg Festival in 2010. On the place of the concept of the tragic in the history of German idealism, see Martin Thibodeau, *Hegel et la tragédie grecque* (Rennes: Presses Universitaires de Rennes, 2011).

satisfy the criteria. Aeschylus's *Orestia* and his *Prometheus Bound* also fit quite well, so long as the concept is somewhat broadened.

In fact, the real problem is with Euripides. Philosophers of the tragic have always recognized as much: as we have seen, many of Euripides's plays do not at all suit the conceptual framework these thinkers sought to define. For the youngest of our three authors is a poor fit within the trio: his dramas have a looser structure, his plots end on a less gloomy note, and his work features a more pronounced expression of feelings. This problem needed to be circumvented. To do so, an explanatory narrative of the evolution of the tragic was produced, claiming that the germ of the tragic is found in a raw and archaic form in Aeschylus, while Sophocles offers it in its fullness and maturity. As for Euripides, he would be identified with the genre's inevitable decadence – Schlegel reproaches him for having destroyed the 'essence' (*inneres Wesen*) of tragedy. According to Nietzsche, Euripides became the destroyer of tragedy.[35] What a lovely little story. Or rather, fable, for what it relates is more like the growth of a fruit, which one can see emerging on a tree, ripening, then rotting, than like that of an actual literary genre. It is certainly not the history of tragedy, which is entirely different.

This Romantic notion of tragedy is all the more paradoxical in that it radically conflicts with the Aristotelian interpretation. While the philosophers of Jena see tragedy inexorably moving away from its essence, the *Poetics* claims on the contrary that it is gradually drawing closer: Aristotle liked to define Euripides as 'the most tragic of the poets'[36]

---

35   A. W. von Schlegel, *Vorlesungen über Ästhetik I* [1798–1803], ed. Ernst Behler (Paderborn: Schöningh, 1989) 747; Nietzsche, *Birth of Tragedy*, 77–86 (chs 11–12). See also Hegel, *Aesthetics*, vol. 2, 1215 and 1221 (3rd part, s. III, ch. III, III, C, 3, c–546 and 554).

36   Aristotle, *Poetics*, ch. XIII, 1453 a 29–30.

(*tragikôtatos tôn poiêtôn*), the one in whose work the essence of tragedy was most clearly displayed. Though tragedy according to Aristotle does not correspond with the German Romantics' definition of the tragic, such a divergence of perspectives raises questions. It suggests one should approach the history of the genre as suggested by the moderns with some scepticism.

Of course, this history was opportunistically simplified by the reduction of the corpus of Attic tragedy to three authors, when the practice of this theatre neither began with Aeschylus nor ended with Euripides. No matter: three tragedians are perfect for defining a beginning, a middle, and an end, even though we are aware that this reduction is only the result of the vagaries of the manuscript tradition and though we also know the names of numerous other authors of tragedies whose works have not reached us: Thespis, Phrynichus, Pratinas, Choerilus, Philocles, Xenocles, Agathon, Euphorion, Ion of Chios, and Critias, to name only a few. Had these authors' works been preserved, it would have been difficult to schematize the history of the genre: critics and philosophers were fortunately spared this effort by the gaps in the transmission of manuscripts.

Yet three authors were still too many. Further simplification was required, and ultimately achieved by arranging the three playwrights chronologically in a linear succession: Aeschylus, then Sophocles, and finally Euripides. A deceptive sequence: while Aeschylus is indisputably the eldest, the twelve final years of his life coincide with the rise of Sophocles. Most importantly, Euripides's career was only a decade away from being contemporary to that of the author of *Oedipus Rex*. Additionally, Sophocles briefly outlived Euripides, and it is he, not Euripides, who among the three great tragedians wrote the most recent tragedy, *Oedipus at Colonus*. If tragedy was beginning its decline at the time of Euripides, it was no less in decline when Sophocles was active, since it was exactly the same period: to sideline Euripides from the great tragic tradition cannot be justified on purely historical or chronological grounds.

As a last resort, some have turned to Euripides's actual career to explain the eccentric nature of his theatre compared to that of his two colleagues, and its relative incompatibility with the idea of the tragic. One exegete boldly states that there were 'two Euripides', one who wrote tragedies and another who gave up tragedy for 'fanciful drama'.[37]

The hypothesis is admittedly seductive, but does one really find such an evolution in Euripides's work? It is highly doubtful. Some of Euripides's most clearly tragic plays – *Phoenician Women* and *Bacchae* – date from the very end of his career. On the other hand, *Alcestis*, one of the most atypical tragedies, is the earliest of his preserved works. As for the other plays, most have been dated in an extremely hypothetical way, more or less determined by critics' vision of the playwright's literary development. Based on such an incomplete and unconvincing chronology, it is difficult to present a picture of Euripides as the apostate of tragedy whose career allegedly saw him move away from a genre he considered archaic to invent a form of theatre regarded as more modern.

The Tragic Corpus: History of a Disaster and a Betrayal

The theory of the 'two Euripides' raises a more fundamental problem. It presupposes that we know how to distinguish between two categories of tragedies: the standard, or strictly tragic, tragedies, and those that are not. Yet do we really know what a normal tragedy was in fifth-century-BCE Athens? It would be a great mistake to think that reading all

---

37   The French term is '*drame romanesque*'. André Rivier, *Essai sur le tragique d'Euripide* [1944] (Paris: De Boccard, 1975), 129–38 and 163–8.

the plays by the great tragedians would suffice to impart a picture of the average tragedy. Besides the fact that we only know three of the dozens of playwrights active during the period, we do not even have access to the complete works of those three. Only a fraction remain. Of the roughly 90 plays composed by Aeschylus, only 7 have survived. Sophocles is thought to have composed 123 plays: as with Aeschylus, only 7 are still extant, along with the fragments of a satyr play. In this regard, Euripides has been the most fortunate, with 19 plays preserved, including 1 satyr play and 1 which is probably apocryphal, of a total of 92. In other words, a total of 32 tragedies out of the 220 written by these three authors (excluding satyr plays).

This figure also needs to be related to the total production of tragedies in Athens during the period. It can easily be calculated that between 472, when Aeschylus staged *The Persians*, and 401, when *Oedipus at Colonus* was performed posthumously, no fewer than 648 tragedies were performed in Athens during the City Dionysia, not counting the satyr plays, a figure to which one should add all the tragedies performed during less important festivals such as the Lenaia and all those that were staged outside Athens – while recognizing, of course, that the history of Greek tragedy does not start in 472 nor stop in 401.[38] In total, well under 5 per cent of the production of tragedies in ancient Greece has come down to us: all the rest is outside our ken, except for a handful of fragments and summaries that scarcely convey a reliable sense of the works they relate to. It is a disaster of dizzying proportions. Even an iceberg reveals more of itself.

Given these facts, how can we imagine what a standard tragedy was like in Athens in the fifth century BCE? With less

---

38 This estimate is based on the fact that three competitors faced off at the City Dionysia, each of whom presented a trilogy of tragedies as well as a satyr play.

than a twentieth of the corpus preserved, is there any guarantee that the plays of Euripides we traditionally consider atypical do not in fact fit the mould of the average tragedy staged during that period? How can we be sure that, on the contrary, it was not the tragedies now judged characteristic of the tragic that were, in their time, out of the ordinary? These are crucial questions, that determine both what place to give to Euripides's allegedly abnormal tragedies and, in the last instance, whether or not it is possible to sum up the idea of tragedy by the concept of the tragic.

The usual answer to these questions is well known: it assumes, on the one hand, that the three poets whose work has survived are characteristic of all the playwrights of their time, and on the other, that we have preserved a sufficiently representative part of their output, despite the enormity of the losses. After all, does not a very small sample of a given population serve to yield highly reliable polls? But to achieve this, the sample must be selected completely at random.

As it happens, the transmission of the tragic works to our era has been anything but random. The choice of the three great tragic poets was made early on. From the fourth century BCE, Aeschylus, Sophocles and Euripides were hailed in Athens as the premier playwrights: the statesman Lycurgus had bronze statues of them raised in the theatre of Dionysus and ordered a master copy of their works to be kept in the public archives, which copy was deposited at the Library of Alexandria one century later. This was a decisive act. Though other poets, such as Agathon and Ion of Chios, continued to be read at least until the first century AD, the pre-eminence granted to the three greats was never questioned again. Today we find ourselves in thrall to an initial selection made in Athens more than 2,000 years ago.

A second selection, generally dated to the second century AD, further consolidated the first: in this era, scholarly and academic circles produced an anthology featuring seven tragedies by Aeschylus, seven by Sophocles, and ten by Euripides. Once copied and circulated, this anthology saved most of what we know about Attic tragedy.[39]

---

[39] The seven plays by Aeschylus are, probably in this order, *Prometheus Bound, Seven against Thebes, The Persians*, the *Oresteia* trilogy, including *Agamemnon, The Libation Bearers*, and *The Eumenides*, and *The Suppliants*. Of Sophocles's plays, only the order of the first three is certain: *Ajax, Electra, Oedipus Rex, Antigone, Oedipus at Colonus, The Women of Trachis* and *Philoctetes*. As for the ten plays by Euripides, the order is as follows: *Hecuba, Orestes, Phoenician Women, Hippolytus, Medea, Alcestis, Andromache, Rhesus, The Trojan Women*, and *Bacchae*. The hypothesis of a selection made in the second century was first put forward, after Theodor Barthold, by Wilamowitz-Moellendorff, who explains the reasons for which the plays were selected in *Einleitung in die griechische Tragödie*, 195–219. The date and specific composition of the selection of plays by Euripides were contested by André Tuilier, *Rechèrches critiques sur la tradition du texte d'Euripide* (Paris: Klincksieck, 1968), 88–113: in particular, Tuilier dates the moment of the selection to the fifth century AD. Leighton Durham Reynolds and Nigel Guy Wilson are quite guarded about Wilamowitz's hypothesis (notably his attribution of the selection to a single man) and agree with Tuilier to date the period of the selection as late as possible, in *Scribes and Scholars: A Guide to the Transmission of Greek and Latin Literature* (Oxford: Clarendon Press, 3rd ed., 1991), 53–4. On the other hand, dating the selection to the second century is supported by new arguments by Jean Irigoin, who makes use of a comparative analysis of Egyptian literary papyri in *La Tradition des textes grecs: Pour une critique historique* (Paris: Belles Lettres, 2003), 162–7. For an overview of the history of the transmission of the Greek tragedians, see Jacques Jouanna, *Sophocle* (Paris: Fayard, 2007), 524–31. In sum, no one denies that a choice was made: the only debate concerns the date at which it was made and its exact content (there are doubts regarding two or three plays by Euripides). Irigoin's position seems the most reasonable. Indeed, those who think the date of the selection is too early base their argument on citations of plays outside the selection found in authors dating from after the second century: according to them, this proves that the selection had not yet been made. But, in fact, no one can deny that the selection's influence on the most cultivated categories of the population was slow and that for centuries educated people had access to anthologies of citations and libraries that contained, if not the complete works, at least a large selection of plays by the three tragedians. Their citations from these plays therefore do not prove anything regarding whether or not a narrower selection was in effect in education. However, what is far more conclusive is the increasing scarcity beginning in the third century of papyri featuring plays outside of the selection, in so far as the Egyptian papyri are a more accurate reflection of the state of popular culture in a certain era.

The fact is that we only have access to Greek tragedy through a selection made in the Roman era by grammarians whose sole focus was on what would be of interest to their students. To highlight this situation's absurdity, let us reverse the perspective: if, around the year 4400, our distant descendants' knowledge of our twentieth- and twenty-first-century literature was not derived from our own choices, but from some kind of literary primer put together in 2638, how much confidence could we have in our descendants' interpretations and judgements? Happily, we will not be around to be outraged.

A selection made under such conditions is affected by numerous factors – whether pedagogical, aesthetic, moral, philosophical, religious, political, or generally ideological – but, under no circumstances, can it claim to present an objective reflection of reality, which could only be achieved by random choice. The editors of the anthology might have chosen the texts they preferred, or those tradition preferred, or the easiest, or the least shocking, or even, as we earnestly wish to believe, the most representative of the diversity of all tragedies. Or all of the above. The problem is that we will never know, because this selection was not delivered to us with an introductory text or a user's manual. It is probable, but no more than that, that the selection corresponded to criteria of a primarily pedagogical nature, allowing for references to the Homeric canon, for the level of difficulty to gradually increase from one play to the next, and for parallels to be established between the three authors' works.[40] For the rest, we are left with pure conjecture: either hoping that these twenty-four tragedies afford a faithful view of the hundreds of tragedies produced in that period, or, on the

---

40 Wilamowitz-Moellendorff, in *What Is an Attic Tragedy?*, and Tuilier, in *Recherches critiques*, provide substantial analyses of the pedagogical motives guiding these choices.

contrary, refusing to put any trust in such an arbitrarily composed group of works. The debate about the tragic remains open: we are likely never to know whether Euripides really did stray from the normal framework of tragedy.

What We Can Learn from Euripides's 'Alphabetic' Tragedies

Except that we are not limited to the twenty-four tragedies mentioned above. In fact, we have access to no fewer than thirty-two plays: on top of the twenty-four selected, we must consider another eight, all of which were outside the original selection and written by Euripides. The extraordinary story of these plays' preservation is all the more deserving of our attention as it has crucial consequences for the issue at hand.

In fact, some medieval manuscripts feature nine additional plays by Euripides alongside the ten included in the selection. Unlike the others, these nine plays are presented without scholia. They have the particularity of being arranged more or less according to the initial of their Greek titles: epsilon for *Helen*; eta for *Electra, Heracles*, and *Heracleidae*; kappa for *Cyclops*; and iota for *The Suppliants* (*Hiketides*), *Ion, Iphigenia in Tauris*, and *Iphigenia in Aulis*. A strange order, but which can be explained by the idea that it roughly reproduces the alphabetical order of an ancient edition of the works of Euripides, of which a partial reproduction, from the medieval period, still existed in Thessaloniki in the fourteenth century. This manuscript has since been lost, but two fourteenth-century copies survive in Rome and Florence.[41] Now we find ourselves with nine additional

---

41 This is the hypothesis of Wilamowitz-Moellendorff, borrowed by Louis Méridier in the introduction to his edition of Euripides, *Le Cyclope, Alceste, Médée, Les Héraclides* (Paris: Belles Lettres, 1976) (1st ed., 1926), xx–xxxi, whose general outlines are on the whole accepted. According to

plays, eight of them tragedies, miraculously rediscovered after having nearly disappeared into the black hole of history. The tradition of Greek and Latin texts is full of these happy or unhappy accidents – most often unhappy, alas, though the details remain unknown; we can only guess that these accidents happened because they would explain why so little of ancient literature has been saved.

Eight tragedies are not many compared to the mass of all the tragedies produced in Athens, or even to those composed only by Euripides. Yet one should not underestimate the exceptional importance of the eight so-called alphabetic plays, which, through a rare combination of factors, form a body of documents entirely outside the academic selection: these are not plays arbitrarily selected for reasons that mostly escape us, but tragedies preserved in an essentially random manner, by alphabetical order. This makes an enormous

---

Alexander Turyn (*The Byzantine Manuscript Tradition of the Tragedies of Euripides* [Urbana: University of Illinois Press, 1957], 222–306 and, more specifically, 241–2 and 303–6), the original manuscript (or its source) was initially in the possession of the great Byzantine grammarian Eustathius of Thessalonica (twelfth century); the Florence copy, made by the scribe Nicolaus Triclines, was revised by his relative, the philologist Demetrius Triclinius, in the fourteenth century. See also Günther Zuntz, *An Inquiry into the Transmission of the Plays of Euripides* (Cambridge: Cambridge University Press, 1965), 276–8; François Jouan, 'Notice', in Euripide, *Iphigénie à Aulis* (Paris: Belles Lettres, 1990), 52–5; Jean Irigoin, *Tradition et critique des textes grecs* (Paris: Belles Lettres, 1997), 129–37; and *Le Poète grec au travail* (Paris: Académie des Inscriptions et Belles-Lettres, 2009), 335–6. According to Bruno Snell ('Zwei Töpfe mit Euripides-Papyri', *Hermes* 70 [1935]: 119–20), an ancient case (*teukhos*) contained five rolls, that is to say five plays gathered alphabetically. The very first Byzantine copyist is thought to have had access to two of these cases, but to have had to exclude *Hecuba*, which was already in the traditional selection; this explains why there are nine surviving alphabetic plays, and not ten. Tuilier, in *Recherches critiques*, 114–27, contests the idea that the alphabetic plays date back to a complete edition of Euripides; he suggests that they offer instead fragmentary evidence of an edition from late Antiquity tasked with completing the plays in the initial selection. In every scenario, one thing is certain: this edition contained a vast selection of Euripides's plays and was necessarily more representative of the poet's general production.

difference: here at last is the control sample we need for a more objective knowledge of Euripides's tragedies.

Comparing the alphabetic tragedies and those of the selection is indeed enlightening. A glance at the list of the alphabetic tragedies reveals that it contains the plays generally considered the most atypical within the tragic corpus, and particularly in Euripides's body of work: *Helen*, *Ion*, and *Iphigenia in Tauris*, notably, but also *Electra* and *Iphigenia in Aulis*. More specifically, of the eight alphabetic tragedies, only one has a fatal ending: *Heracles*. One finds the opposite proportion among the ten plays in the selection, of which only two have a happy ending: *Orestes* and *Alcestis* (in fact, *Alcestis* does not quite belong among the ordinary tragedies, since it served as a satyr play). It would be difficult to achieve a more flagrant contrast.

The difference between the two groups yields a wealth of insights. We have seen that in the modern era, Euripides is considered as the least tragic of these writers. In fact, of the seventeen extant tragedies attributed to him, outside of *Alcestis*, only nine have an unhappy ending, or 53 per cent. There is no doubt that this relatively low proportion has contributed to relegating the playwright to a position below that of the great tragedians. But as we have just seen, this low ratio is merely an artefact of the manuscript tradition, which mixes two radically distinct families of plays: one determined arbitrarily, comprising 89 per cent of unhappy endings, and the other purely random, and only containing 12 per cent of unhappy endings.[42]

---

42 Without *Alcestis*, 89 per cent of the plays in the selection have unhappy endings; with *Alcestis*, the rate is 80 per cent. The argument can be completed if we take into account the numerous fragments of Euripides's tragedies that have been found and were published in a remarkable edition by François Jouan and Herman Van Looy, in Euripide, *Tragédies, Vol. VIII: Fragments* (Paris: Belles Lettres, 2002–03), 4 vols. If we only consider the tragedies whose plot and ending can be reconstructed with sufficient certainty, there are six tragedies with unhappy endings out

In other words, if we had not preserved the alphabetic plays, which are very likely to be more representative of the playwright's whole oeuvre, Euripides would not appear to us as the least tragic, but the *most tragic* author of trage-dies, being the most inclined to give his plays an unhappy ending. This is obviously an absurd hypothesis, since the alphabetic tragedies fortunately do exist. Yet not so absurd as not to afford us a better understanding, by inference, of the particular situation of the two other playwrights, Aeschylus and Sophocles. For these two authors appear to us in exactly that configuration: all that we have left of their work are the plays from the selection. Contrary to Euripi-des, we have no access to their tragedies ignored by the academic tradition. With this in mind, it does not take much of a leap to believe that knowledge of plays by Aeschylus and Sophocles outside of the selection would radically alter our perception of their art, in proportions as significant as it has with Euripides. This hypothesis must at least force us to put everything we thought we knew about Attic tragedy into perspective, lest the tragedies generally considered as models of the genre prove to be exceptions. And this is exactly what the study of the transmission of Euripides's texts reveals.

---

of twenty-three, or only 26 per cent. Here is a detailed breakdown: the tragedies with unhappy endings are *Bellerophon*, *Erechtheus*, *Hippolytus Veiled*, *Meleager*, *Protesilaus* and *Stheneboea*; those with non-unhappy endings are *Alexander*, *Alcmaeon*, *Alope*, *Andromeda*, *Antigone*, *Antiope*, *Archelaus*, *Danae*, *Melanippe Captive*, *Oeneus*, *Polyidus*, *Scyrians*, *Telephus*, *Hypsipyle*, *Philoctetes*, *Phoenix* and *Phrixus*. These statistics, which obviously do not take into account the satyr plays, must nonetheless be approached with caution, given that reconstructing plots from mere fragments or summaries remains questionable. For example, if we choose to include in this count other tragedies whose unhappy ending is probable, though disputable in the current state of documentation, namely *Oedipus*, *Palamedes*, *Phaethon* and *Chrysippus*, we would have ten tragedies with unhappy endings out of a total of twenty-seven, or 37 per cent. In any case, these results confirm what is revealed by the analysis of the alphabetic tragedies.

This imparts a few major lessons. First of all, that it is necessary to re-evaluate Euripides's place among the three tragedians: if one wants to make a proper comparison of the poet and his colleagues, one should only take into account the plays included in the selection, in order to consider him in a position equivalent to that of Aeschylus and Sophocles. Any other approach would be a distortion, since it is perfectly possible that Sophocles's lost plays were as different from his seven canonical tragedies as Euripides's alphabetical plays are from those in the selection. On the other hand, if we only consider the latter and not the alphabetical tragedies, then the differences between Sophocles and Euripides immediately and strikingly diminish.

Forget *Oedipus Rex*

That long-ago selection of tragedies manifestly served as a Procrustean bed by privileging plays that had common characteristics. One thing is clear: if we are to judge by Euripides's case, the plays in the selection match the modern concept of the tragic more closely than those that were left out. How do we explain this curious situation?

One cannot simply say that the best plays were selected, and that *ipso facto* these also happened to be the most tragic: we know how crucial it is to break this hermeneutical circle. In fact, the plays considered the most successful in the second century AD were not always the ones that had the most success six centuries earlier. Euripides's *Helen* and *Iphigenia in Tauris*, today considered among the most atypical tragedies, were not part of the selection but were nonetheless among the playwright's most popular.[43] Even more incredible:

---

43   See Henri Grégoire's notes in Euripide, *Hélène* (Paris: Belles Lettres, 1985), 40, and *Iphigénie en Tauride* (Paris: Belles Lettres, 1982), 106.

Oedipus Rex, the ultimate model of the tragedy, ranked first by Aristotle and often considered the absolute masterpiece of the form,[44] only received second prize at the contest.[45] Admittedly, the prize was attributed to a tetralogy, not individual tragedies, and the other plays that composed the tetralogy are unknown to us. Which did not prevent the second-century AD rhetorician Aelius Aristides from venting his outrage over this injustice:

> Before an Athenian audience Philocles defeated Sophocles and his *Oedipus*, O Zeus and ye gods! *Oedipus*, against whom not even Aeschylus could say anything. Then on this account was Sophocles inferior to Philocles? In truth, even proclaiming Sophocles better than Philocles would have been an insult to him.[46]

There is every indication that the criteria for assessing tragedy were turned upside down over the course of six centuries. And why not? Aesthetic transformations of the sort are the rule. The unfortunate thing is that we are still dependent on this judgement made six centuries after the golden age of tragedy. Despite the fact that it is far from certain that Athenians preferred this type of tragedy, philosophy has taken *Oedipus Rex* as its example of the perfect tragedy, with its concentrated action and an initial situation tautly implying all that ensues, and in which the pleasure lies in

---

44 Aristotle, *Poetics*, XI, 1452 a 32–33; XV, 1454 b 6–8; XVI, 1455 a 16–19; XXVI, 1462 a 18 b 3.

45 See Sophocle, vol. 2: *Ajax, Œdipe roi, Électre* (Paris: Belles Lettres, 1989), 66 and 69.

46 Aelius Aristides, *Pros Platôna: Huper tôn tettarôn* [To Plato: In defence of the four], 256, 11 (422), in the W. Dindorf edition (Leipzig: Weidmann, 1829), vol. 2, 334; quoted by Jouanna, *Sophocle*, 98. This English translation is adapted from P. Aelius Aristides, *The Complete Works: Volume 1. Orations I–XVI*, trans. Charles A. Behr (Leiden: E. J. Brill, 1986), Oration III, 239.

seeing one event lead to the next in an almost mechanical fashion. Many other plays, including *Helen*, *The Trojan Women*, *The Phoenician Women*, and even *Oedipus at Colonus*, do not fit this blueprint of the compressed plot and consist instead of a series of relatively disconnected scenes. To understand tragedy, we also need to consider these plays, which were no less successful in their time than Sophocles's masterpiece and may even have been far more popular. The time has come to stop thinking of tragedy according to the model of *Oedipus Rex*, to shift paradigms and give the thoroughly anachronistic concept of the tragic a well-deserved rest.

A Selection of Tragedies Inspired by the Stoics

Maurice Bowra, one of the twentieth century's most famous Hellenists, was taken aback to observe that Sophocles's tragedies were less tragic than those of Shakespeare. He was indignant that the critics of Antiquity could admire the beauty of Sophocles's poetry while saying 'nothing of his tragic vision or his conception of life'. Dio Chrysostom and Pseudo-Longinus, for instance, heaped praise on the poet but did not say a word about his philosophical and religious side.[47] And with good reason, one is tempted to respond: the tragic as we know it did not exist for the ancient writers. In the golden century of Attic tragedy, the concept was unknown and hence devoid of operational value.

In *Thesmophoriazusae* and *The Frogs*, Aristophanes aims countless barbs at Euripides for his poetry, music, and type of character, but never for the construction of the plot itself: though he spared Euripides nothing, the great comic

---

47 Cecil Maurice Bowra, *Sophoclean Tragedy* (Oxford: Clarendon Press, 1944), 357 and 359. Bowra cites Dio Chrysostom, *Discourses, LII: On Aeschylus, Sophocles and Euripides, or The Bow of Philoctetes*, 17, and the treatise *On the Sublime*, XV, 7; XXIII, 3; XXXIII, 5.

playwright never charges, for example, that he is less *tragic* than Aeschylus or Sophocles. At the time, such an argument would simply have been inconceivable. Yet as we have seen, close to a century later, Aristotle would describe Euripides as 'the most tragic of the poets' – not in the modern sense of the word, but in the sense of *the one who makes the best use of the resources of tragedy.*

This discrepancy between the modern vision of tragedy and antique reality can easily be explained: what is today referred to as *tragic* is merely an epiphenomenon of the performance of ancient tragedies; it was not a goal in and of itself. It only appears intermittently, in some of the tragedies – not the majority, and not necessarily in those that were most successful in their time.

This is particularly true of the idea of fate. It appears as early as Homer and is very present in Greek thought and literature under various, not entirely synonymous names: *anankê* is necessity; *tuchê* is fortune; *moira* is fate; *heimarmenê* is destiny itself, namely the *fatum* of the Latins and so on.[48] Yet, while this nebula of concepts can be found everywhere in the texts, it does not play a central, structuring role in philosophy before the third century BCE, when Zeno of Citium developed his reflection on fate. Countless books followed on the same subject, by authors including Epicurus, Chrysippus, Boethus of Sidon, Clitomachus, Philopator,

---

48 One could mention even more near synonyms: *aisa, pepromenê, potmos, khreôn* etc. On the concept of fate in tragedy, notably see Wilhelm Gundel, *Beiträge zur Entwickelungsgeschichte der Begriffe Ananke und Heimarmene* (Brühl: Giessen, 1914), 34–9. Gundel is also the author of the article on 'Heimarmene' in *Paulys Realencyclopädie der classischen Altertumswissenschaft* (Munich: Druckenmüller, 1912), vol. VII-2, col. 2622–45. In the same encyclopaedia, it is also useful to consult the articles on 'Moira' and 'Tyche'. Despite the title of his book (*L'idea di destino nel pensiero antico* [Udine: Del Bianco, 1984], vol. 1, 139–243), Aldo Magris puts forward a conception of fate far less anchored in the ancient categories than in German Romantic and post-Romantic philosophy.

Diogenianus, Posidonius, Cicero, Plutarch, and Alexander of Aphrodisias, to name but a few. This was the birth of Stoicism, and all the polemics that came with it.

As it happens, the concept of the tragic, particularly in the sense given by Schelling, is not conceivable without the existence or pre-existence of Stoic doctrine – that is, of a system in which fate plays a central part. Admittedly, the great authors of tragedies made supernatural forces intervene in their characters' lives and included many of the oracles that were so present in everyday Greek life, but there is nothing to indicate that they were primarily interested in the role of fate: their plots account for realities specific to their world (of which the oracles were obviously a part), but these realities do not set the fundamental tone for their work nor serve as the plot's dramatic or philosophical driving force. From this point of view, it is highly significant that none of Aeschylus, Sophocles, Euripides nor any of the other authors of tragedies whose fragments have been preserved use the term *heimarmenê*, though they undoubtedly knew it: this is not what they wanted to put at the heart of their tragedies.

We believe otherwise only through an error of perspective and a historical betrayal. If several surviving plays by Aeschylus, Sophocles and Euripides appear to magnificently illustrate the idea of fate – and who could deny it? – it is because they have primarily reached us through a selection made around the second century AD. During this period, the influence of Stoicism achieved an unrivalled significance in the Greco-Latin world, ranging to the greatest heights of power: the emperor Marcus Aurelius made Stoicism his personal philosophy; Stoic concepts became commonplace and spread to all the schools of philosophy; and, in particular, the ideas of fate and providence became infinitely more important than they were at the time of the great tragedians. It is not insignificant that the Stoics liked to cite *Oedipus*

Rex to explain the power of fatality:[49] the second-century selection clearly reflects this preference for works that could echo the philosophical concerns of the moment. Conversely, it is revealing that Euripides's alphabetic tragedies, which are entirely separate from this selection, do not so easily fit into the conceptual framework of Stoicism: they show that the field of tragedy was far more diverse, aesthetically and ideologically, than is suggested by the plays chosen by educators of the early Christian era, and offer a glimpse of a radically different world than the one presented in the tragedies canonized by tradition. To compare the plays in the selection and the alphabetic plays is to bring two nearly irreconcilable worlds face to face.

Tragedy as a Theatrical Revue

So, what was tragedy? We will probably never know. But it is likely that the authors sought less to stage an idea, even less a philosophical idea such as man's oppression by fate,

---

49 See Cicero, who cites the Stoic Chrysippus in *On Fate*, XIII–30; Alexander of Aphrodisias, *On Fate*, 31. Chrysippus set out his arguments based not only on the story of Oedipus, but also on Euripides's tragedies, *Medea* and *The Phoenician Women*: see Jean-Baptiste Gourinat, 'Prédiction du futur et action humaine dans le traité de Chrysippe *Sur le destin*', in *Les Stoïciens*, dir. Gilbert Romeyer Dherbey, ed. J.-B. Gourinat (Paris: Vrin, 2005), 270–3. With the exception of *Hercules furens*, the Latin tragedies written by Seneca also confirm the Stoic predilection for a certain type of tragedy with an unhappy ending. On the Stoic influence during the imperial period, see Max Pohlenz, *Die Stoa: Geschichte einer geistigen Bewegung* [1948] (Göttingen: Vandenhoeck & Ruprecht, 7th ed., 1992), 354–66; Giovanni Reale, *Storia della filosofia antica* (1975–80), vol. 4: *Le scuole dell'età imperiale* (Milan: Vita e Pensiero, 8th ed., 1994), 73–148; Christopher Gill, 'The School in the Roman Imperial Period', in *The Cambridge Companion to the Stoics*, ed. Brad Inwood (Cambridge: Cambridge University Press, 2003), 33–58 (particularly on the concept of fate in Latin poetry, 57–8). On the decisive role of Stoicism in the spread of the concepts of fate and providence, see Pierre Thillet, 'Introduction', in Alexander of Aphrodisias, *Traité du destin* (Paris: Belles Lettres, 1984), lxxxii–xc; *Traité de la Providence* (Lagrasse: Verdier, 2003), 30–42.

than to bring before the public a hero or a god. The analogy with Noh drama as described by Claudel still works quite fruitfully here: Greek tragedy is not about something that happens, but someone who arrives. It is Oedipus arriving at Colonus before the astounded Athenian audience, Helen appearing on the banks of the Nile, and Xerxes returning to his palace in Susa. The embodiment of the character is primarily in his mask, not in his actions.

It therefore follows that contrary to Aristotelian theory and common opinion, drama does not come first in tragedy. The *Poetics* only focuses on the action as an object of analysis and speculation, while taking little interest in the actual mechanism of tragic embodiment. To read that 'Tragedy . . . is an imitation of an action' (*mimêsis praxeôs*) or that 'people acting realize the imitation' (*prattontes poiountai tên mimêsin*)[50] is to understand that there is an action on stage that is an imitation of another action offstage, which is past or fictional. Yet does the action actually carry the full weight of imitation on its own, as the philosopher claims? All things considered, if tragedy is the 'imitation of an action', it is more because it resembles an action without actually being one. Imitation does not take place through action, but through *presence*.

In fact, the entire action is already contained in the character, in the well-known story or myth the character sums up solely by his appearance and mask. The tragedy merely uses the time of the performance to unfold a reality that is already there, before the eyes and in the minds of the audience. The fourth-century-BCE comic poet Antiphanes explained as much in a richly ironic passage:

Tragedy is a marvellous genre in every way, since from the outset its subjects are known to the audience, before anyone

50 Aristotle, *Poetics*, ch. VI, 1449 b 24 and 31.

has even opened his mouth, so that the poet merely needs to remind us of them. I name Oedipus and they know all the rest: that his father is Laius, his mother Jocasta, who his sons and daughters are, what will happen to him and what he has done. Likewise, if we name Alcmaeon, we have named all his children, we know that in a moment of madness he killed his mother and that indignant Adrastus will come at once, then leave again . . . Then when the poets, no longer knowing what to say, throw in the towel in the middle of the drama, they set in motion the theatre machine as easily as they move their little finger, and the audience is happy.[51]

What Antiphanes expresses in a satirical mode must be taken seriously: tragedy begins by presenting a character, and all the rest follows, because one specific character entails a specific legend, another character a specific place, a specific plot and so on. Consequently, tragedy does not initially appear as an action, but as a series of scenes drawn from a legend, which the author more or less artfully coordinates. *Prometheus Bound*, *The Phoenician Women* and *The Trojan Women* function like revue performances, with basically disconnected numbers separated by periodic singing appearances from the chorus. This is also true of *Oedipus at Colonus*. Oedipus merely needs to arrive on stage for the various members of his family to appear one after the other, as if by magic, each entitled to one memorable scene: Ismene, Creon, and finally Polynices – a veritable parade of the Labdacids and their allies.

What we call *scenes* often come down to the succession of required moments borrowed from the myth: mere clichéd images. Yes, the author can potentially focus on some dramatic

---

51 Antiphanes, fragment 189, in *Poetae comici Graeci*, ed. Rudolf Kassel and Colin Austin (Berlin: De Gruyter, 1991), vol. 2, 418; cited by Jouanna, *Sophocle*, 135. Translation based on Jouanna.

or psychological coherence between the different scenes, but he is not bound to do so. And since the hero's life is a given from the outset, the impression is produced of an entire life determined by fate, and of a hero struggling against that fate. This is however an ill-founded or, at the very least, excessive interpretation. Wilamowitz said so long ago, with his customary precision: '[The poets] invoked fate, which in truth was only an expression to indicate the constraints of the legend that weighed on the poet.'[52] In fact, the primary function of the various oracles in *Oedipus at Colonus* is to serve as pretexts for the appearance of different characters.

Is it shocking to describe tragedy as a revue worthy of the music hall? It is certainly no more inaccurate than the tragic model commonly applied to these plays, a model we eventually have to let go, along with so many other ideas. Perhaps these were not devoid of interest: stimulating, fascinating, brilliant ideas. But mere ideas, nonetheless, such as this 'tragic' as versatile as it is impertinent, sneaking back in through the window when we thought we had chased it out the door. Tragedies were not tragic. They were something other, but we will never know what: that is the only absolute certainty that emerges from the history of their ideologically biased transmission.

---

52 Wilamowitz-Moellendorff, *What Is an Attic Tragedy?*, 225 (*Einleitung in die griechische Tragödie*, 118).

Third, Fourth, and Fifth Episodes

Terror and Pity

As the inhabitants of Colonus are celebrating the beauty and power of Athens, the man whose arrival they have dreaded suddenly appears: Creon, followed by an armed escort. He invites Oedipus to return to Thebes. In response to the old blind man's obstinate refusal, and despite the Athenians' intervention, Creon has Ismene and Antigone abducted.

Called to the rescue, Theseus hurries back. While Creon reaffirms his own rights over Oedipus before the king of Athens, the blind man justifies himself for all the crimes of which he is accused: did he commit a single one on purpose? Theseus decides to take Creon back to the border and sends his men to bring back the two captive women.

Left alone with Oedipus, the people of Colonus imagine the battle against the Thebans to free the prisoners. Theseus soon returns, accompanied by the two young women. A moving reunion with their father. But now the arrival of a supplicant is announced: it is the oldest son, Polynices. Oedipus reluctantly agrees to listen to him. Theseus leaves.

Enter Polynices. With six allies, he has raised an army to re-conquer the throne of Thebes and now begs his father to take his side. Oedipus initially declines to answer, then decides to do so at the insistence of the inhabitants of Colonus. But he speaks only to accuse his two sons of having driven him from the palace, and to solemnly curse them: the *two unworthy sons can hope for no other lot than to kill each other in combat. Polynices is stricken. Only Antigone shows him her pity. He immediately leaves to meet his army and his fate.*

3

The Body

In memoriam Jacob Bernays (1824–1881)

Deprived of place, tragedy finds itself unmoored.[1] It wanders like a lost soul, tossed back and forth between contradictory interpretations. Each wants to restore its vanished raison d'être; each has legitimate claims to do so; none completely succeeds. The illusion of a justification regained cannot survive close inspection.

So it goes with the tragic. It was a beautiful idea, one of the most beautiful conceptual efforts launched by philosophy in the last centuries. In this respect, the attempt deserves our admiration. But the tragic thing about the tragic, so to speak, is that it does not measure up to the diversity of the texts. For there is not *one* tragic: there are nearly as many as there are tragedies, and barely fewer than there are philosophers.

More problematic still is that, fascinating though it is, the idea of the tragic is entirely foreign to tragedy, because one must also take into account those tragedies that are not in the least tragic. Admittedly, these are not always the most appreciated, read or performed, but they present an annoying inconvenience: that of existing, whether we like it or not. And we do not know exactly how many there were: while

---

1   An abridged version of this chapter appeared under the title 'La véritable *catharsis* aristotélicienne: Pour une lecture philologique et physiologique de la Poétique', *Poétique*, no. 166 (April 2011): 131–54.

non-tragic tragedies only make up a sizable minority of preserved plays, there are strong reasons to believe – as we saw in the previous chapter – that they compose the majority of lost tragedies. There is no denying this is a scandalous hypothesis. But the opposite hypothesis has fewer arguments in its favour.

We must resign ourselves to the fact that we will likely never know if Greek tragedies were in fact tragic. Far from tautological, such a statement is in the realm of the undecidable, or even the improbable – and it will remain there for eternity, unless by some stroke of luck that could only be the product of the kind of miracle encountered in fairy tales and dreams, the entirety of the corpus suddenly reappeared in our libraries. Best not to count on it. So, let us make do with what we have, criticize widely accepted fallacies, and resign ourselves to the unknowable: we will never stare the essence of tragedy in the face.

Aristotle, Post-Tragic Thinker

Once place no longer has a place and even the concept is no longer thinkable, what remains? Only the texts and their effect on us. Admittedly, that is cold comfort. But Aristotle was not much better off: a reader with his roll – or his codex, or his screen – and nothing else.

Strange as it may seem today, the author of the *Poetics* was the first post-tragic thinker. He arrived in Athens in the fourth century, several decades after the deaths of Euripides and Sophocles, at a time when theatrical spectacles had changed a great deal and already had little in common with what is generally called the golden age of tragedy. This was the moment when theatres began to be built of stone rather than wood; when the orchestra pit became rounded to take the shape we now find, for example, in the impressive remains of the theatre at Epidaurus; when the stage (*proskên-ion*), in the strict sense of the term, rose out of the ground; when the canon of authors and works was established; and lastly, when playbills began increasingly to make room for repertory, to the detriment of the staging of new original works, for all that these had been the mainstay of competitions a century earlier. Aristotle did not directly experience the theatre of Aeschylus, Sophocles and Euripides.[2] While there is no doubt that he attended performances, what he saw corresponded only imperfectly to what previous generations had known.

Of course, we should not exaggerate Aristotle's incompetence in this field: as distant as he may have been from the golden age of tragedy, he was infinitely closer to it than we are. Many contemporary scholars of classical tragedy, including those most critical of Aristotelian poetics, would be delighted to see what Aristotle saw, for lack of anything better.

But, ultimately, this is not the point. Whatever the philosopher did or did not see would not have changed the *Poetics* by one iota, since in the final analysis the theatrical performance as such does not much interest the philosopher. He says so on several occasions: 'The Spectacle . . . is connected least with the art of poetry. For the power of Tragedy . . . is felt even apart from representation and actors.' And: '[Tragedy] reveals its power by mere reading.'[3] Plato referred to his

---

2   See Florence Dupont, *Aristote ou le vampire du théâtre occidental* (Paris: Flammarion, 2007), 32–4. Brigitte Le Guen places more emphasis on the continuities between the theatres of the fifth and fourth centuries ('Avant-propos', in *À chacun sa tragédie? Retour sur la tragédie grecque*, ed. Le Guen [Rennes: Presses Universitaires de Rennes, 2007], 9–10).

3   Aristotle, *Poetics*, respectively, VI, 1450 b 17–20 and XXVI, 1462 a 12. See also XIV, 1453 b 3–7. For translation of passages from the *Poetics*, this English edition relies on the translation by S. H. Butcher (New York: Hill & Wang, 1961) with occasional modifications to match the French emphasis.

disciple as 'the reader'. We have had occasion above to regret that the leading ancient thinker on tragedy denied the realities of theatre.[4]

But this is no longer important, and there is no reason to regret anything. On the contrary: if Aristotle matters to us in the twenty-first century, it is precisely because he was the first to experience the situation with which we are now faced. In other words, the permanent loss of the place and the mutation of tragedy. Of course, there is a difference between the philosopher and us: we live with this deprivation because the flight of time and the ruin of things force us to, while Aristotle's stance was largely due to a personal choice – that of only considering tragedy through its text and of limiting his attention to the tragedies that had already entered the repertory. But, beyond this disparity of causes, which provides plenty of topics for meditation, the result is the same. Aristotle is indeed the thinker who will allow us to mourn the realities of tragedy, since this mourning was, in his case, voluntary, while for us it is a matter of obligation and resignation. He shows us the way: he is our precursor and the one to console us.

Aristotle could not care less about *place*: he simply is not interested. As for the *idea*, the philosopher is in a situation analogous to our own, though symmetrical: if we are living after the patent end or failure of the idea of the tragic, he was there before it even emerged. In Aristotle, the tragic is still something vague: he merely offers the first slender signs of it.

Our confusion when faced with Greek tragedy therefore finds some distant equivalent in the author of the *Poetics*. How can we think about tragedy if we no longer have the place to which it was indissolubly bound? More to the point, how can we think about it if the thought itself is taken away

---

4 See Chapters 1 and 2.

from us – in other words, if the idea of the tragic to which the unfathomable diversity of tragedies has often been reduced is recognized as valueless? To this double question – or rather to this question labouring under the double constraints of the end of place and of the idea – Aristotle provides a simple answer, which can be useful to this day. It is expressed in a single word: the reader, or the spectator, or also – but this is virtually the same thing – the body. It is no longer a question of thinking about tragedy, but of feeling its effects in ourselves, however physical they may be. The idea no longer takes first place.

We must, of course, be clear about this downgrading of the idea. It goes without saying that the *Poetics* is an admirable intellectual exercise on the subject of tragedy and poetry. It is a philosopher's treatise: in that respect, thought is in its element there. But it is a philosophical treatise written in a period when the most speculative philosophy always aimed for a practical reform of human existence. Philosophers were teachers of life as much as of truth.[5]

The *Poetics* has too rarely been read in this light; we must stop seeing it as a purely theoretical work. The first sentence says as much: it is a question of thinking not only 'of Poetry in itself and of its various kinds', but also of 'the specific power (*dunamin*) of each'.[6] A crucial sentence: if we neglect it, forgetting that for Aristotle each form of poetry has a particular power or action, which needs to be defined, we run the risk of finding many passages of the *Poetics* obscure for lack of having understood its essential aim.

This would be the case with tragedy, the subject of the greater part of what has reached us of this key treatise: according to Aristotle, one cannot think about tragedy

---

5 See Pierre Hadot, *Qu'est-ce que la philosophie antique?* (Paris: Gallimard, 1995).
6 Aristotle, *Poetics*, I, 1447 a 8–9.

without taking account of its effects on those who read or watch it – effects which, for their part, are not necessarily in the realm of abstract thought. The incomparable speculation that makes up the *Poetics* hangs on something that ultimately defies reason: an impression from reading, the memory of a performance, a singular emotion. Something that resides elsewhere than in the pure operation of the mind, and that we have no choice but to call the *body*: the body of the reader, the body of the spectator, and, first of all, the body of Aristotle himself, as reader or spectator, the subtle point on which the entire edifice rests.

The Enigma of Catharsis

This attention to the body admirably sheds light on the most famous passage of the *Poetics*, the one that has inspired the most commentary over the centuries.

In 1775, the Académie des Sciences permanently banned from its debates any dissertation dealing with doubling the cube, angle trisection, squaring the circle, and perpetual motion. A wise decision. Why have the same strictures not been applied to Aristotelian catharsis? In the entire history of thought and philosophy, few terms have been as thoroughly examined, weighed, and dissected as the two words that close the general definition of tragedy in Chapter VI of the famous treatise: *pathêmatôn katharsin*, 'catharsis of emotions'. The disproportion between the tenuousness of the original material and the mass of scholarly volumes devoted to it is dizzying. But it says a great deal about the huge mutations undergone over the centuries by what we now call literature and about the chasm of misunderstanding that has opened between ancient poetry and us, a chasm so deep that what seemed obvious in the fourth century has now become an enigma.

It is therefore with some qualms that we now set out to propose a new interpretation of catharsis. Well, not exactly new: this approach aspires only to return to the original concept, straying as little as possible from the writings of Aristotle and his school.

This has not always been the case. Each era has spawned its own notion of catharsis. The sixteenth century took the humanist and philological approach, always pushing expertise on the ancient texts to the fore. In true *Grand Siècle* fashion, the seventeenth and eighteenth centuries followed the moral option. The nineteenth and the first half of the twentieth centuries went whole-hog for the medical and physiological interpretation: the triumph of German philology and its academy. The 1970s proposed a structuralist, narratological, and formalist interpretation. The 1990s made it cognitivist, with a dash of gender theory. As for the 2000s, 9/11 led to an attempt to throw everything out and start again: '*Catharsis*, you say? You must have misread: Aristotle never said a word about it.' I will discuss this terrorist operation below. We eagerly await the postcolonial interpretation, which is surely not far off. For catharsis is a catch-all concept, a mirror of the ideology and presuppositions of those who dare to tackle it: it is enough to put you off scholars and even off yourself.[7]

Which is yet another reason to return to the texts and nothing but the texts. Let us say we are following the literary history and philology option, since its return has been announced: if one must rally around a flag, that one is as good as any other.

---

7 On this history of the interpretations of catharsis, see Adnan K. Abdulla, *Catharsis in Literature* (Bloomington: Indiana University Press, 1985); Stephen Halliwell, *Aristotle's Poetics* (London: Duckworth, 1986), 350–6; Barbara Gernez, *Aristote, Poétique* (Paris: Belles Lettres, 1997), 117–23.

Here is the controverted passage:

> Tragedy, then, is an imitation of an action that is serious, complete, and of a certain magnitude; in language embellished with each kind of artistic ornament, the several kinds being found in separate parts of the play; in the form of people in action, not of narrative, [an imitation] effecting through pity and terror the catharsis of such emotions.[8]

Every term of this particularly dense definition refers to previous or subsequent explanations in the treatise and aims to distinguish between tragedy and other literary forms, such as comedy (whose action is not 'serious') and the epic (which only uses 'narrative'). Every term except, alas, those that compose the very last part of the definition, namely: 'the catharsis of such emotions'. Nowhere else, neither before nor after, does the *Poetics* ever mention any such catharsis.[9] This absence is all the more regrettable given that the last part of the definition seems to aim to describe tragedy's ultimate effect, one intimately tied to the body: emotion.

The problem is therefore as simple to formulate as it has been difficult for scholars to resolve: what is this mysterious 'catharsis', for which it is currently premature to provide a translation? It has been seen as so many different and contradictory things over the centuries that contemporary interpreters cannot but feel uncomfortable. To make their contribution to the wonky edifice of interpretations, they have no choice but to repeat the moves of their predecessors: pick up the clues lying here and there, gather them up into a body of evidence, and propose or reiterate the hypothesis that proves the most compatible. Only one thing is clear, and

---

8 Aristotle, *Poetics*, VI, 1449 b 20–21.
9 I am obviously excluding the occurrence in *Poetics*, XVII, 1455 b 15, where *katharsis* refers to 'religious purification' in a context completely unrelated to the 'catharsis of emotions'.

that is the investigation's objective. Like for any detective on a murder case, the first task is to find the body: the body of the reader or the spectator, of course, of the person who has been touched by the tragedy.

The simplest tactic would be to get Aristotle to talk. It seems odd that the chief witness left no other explanation of the power tragedy wielded over the reader or spectator, if it were really so important to him. In fact, further explanation is not totally lacking: while the *Poetics* says nothing about catharsis outside of the passage quoted, one finds a promising allusion to it in another treatise, the *Politics*. Listing the effects of music, the philosopher mentions the term in question, specifying that, 'what we refer to as *catharsis*, we speak of here only in vague terms, but we will speak about it more clearly in the books on poetics'.[10]

This suggests there was a text in which Aristotle set down his thoughts on the matter. Not, clearly, the passage of the *Poetics* cited above, which remains extremely hazy. This is not the only oddity pertaining to the *Poetics*: shortly before his famous definition of tragedy, Aristotle announces that he will later deal with comedy, and yet the rest of the volume barely touches on it.[11] It has long been thought that there must have existed a second, now lost, volume of the *Poetics*, which would account for these mysteries: a volume notably dealing with comedy, and in which the phenomenon of catharsis was presented in detail – unless the *Politics* was referring to an entirely separate work (such as a dialogue on poets, for example). It is also possible that the further discussions Aristotle planned to broach on comedy and catharsis remained unfinished. Or else that the explanation of catharsis in our current version of the *Poetics* was overlooked by a copyist, and subsequent copyists never corrected the oversight.

---

10 Aristotle, *Politics*, VIII, VII, 1341 b 38–40.
11 Aristotle, *Poetics*, VI, 1449 b 20–21.

Or else, finally, that the text was consumed by humidity, rats and maggots. Strabo reports that towards the end of the third century BCE, Aristotle's manuscripts were carelessly piled up in a basement by negligent heirs, before being rediscovered and published one century later.[12] These mishaps may have contributed to entrenching the mystery of catharsis: all it would have taken is one particularly voracious rat.

Today, the *Poetics* is only pored over by bookworms forced to come up with their own theories about catharsis, since Aristotle did not leave us an explanation. Yet we can be sure that much of the mechanism of catharsis was familiar to readers and listeners contemporary to Aristotle. If, on two occasions in the *Poetics* and the *Politics*, the philosopher was satisfied with merely referring to a later explanation, it must mean that no detailed discussion was immediately required for his point to come across. One thing is certain, and can give us hope in this hermeneutical undertaking: the phenomenon of catharsis must, to some extent, be self-evident.

Given the amount of writing that has proliferated around the concept, we must grant that self-evidence does not appear to be its principal property. Yet it is significant that these multiple interpretations only began in the modern era, as if in Antiquity the problem did not exist. Between Antiquity and today, something must have been lost that once made the idea of catharsis relatively banal. Something that had to do with literature, perhaps; with the body, probably; with both, most likely. Not necessarily a particular text, but rather a generally accepted idea, a widely acknowledged presupposition, whose loss over time has made incomprehensible what was once easily grasped without much ado. Seen from this perspective, the current lack of understanding of catharsis reveals the concept's ancient reality, and the

---

12 Strabo, *Geography*, XIII, I, 54 (608–609). See also Plutarch, *Life of Sulla*, 26, 1–3 (468 a-b).

specific history of its reception provides clues to return to the forgotten self-evidence.

Ideally, the search for what has been lost would involve reconstructing the mental universe of one of Aristotle's readers in Antiquity. A daunting task. But returning to the definition of tragedy cited above can help. For the most part, as we have seen, this definition does not raise any unsurmountable problem in terms of comprehension. It consists of a formal description of the object considered, whose nature it specifies: it is an imitation, imitating a specific kind of action, using a specific kind of language, in a specific way and so on.

The only part that really snags is the last segment, which does not allude to formal characteristics but to what tragedy actually achieves: it is an 'imitation . . . effecting through pity and fear the catharsis of such emotions' (*mimêsis . . . di' eleou kai phobou perainousa tên tôn toioutôn pathêmatôn katharsin*). If our hypothesis is correct, namely if this proposition was evident to the ancient readers of Aristotle, all of its terms would necessarily have been clear when considered together, and the meaning of catharsis would be inseparable from that of the other terms surrounding it.

No solution to the problem of catharsis can be valid if it does not simultaneously answer the following questions: Why do pity and terror play a part in the process, and why only them? What does 'such' mean in 'such emotions'? Are they the same emotions (pity and terror), or emotions of the same kind? Does *pathêmatôn* refer to feelings and affections or, as is also possible, to events? Does the genitive used have a subjective, objective, or separative value? Above all, why must catharsis be achieved by an 'imitation' or a 'representation' (*mimêsis*)? The right interpretation of catharsis should enable all these questions to be answered in one fell swoop. In other words, if we find an overall answer to these questions and discover the key that opens all the doors, the nature of catharsis will no longer be a mystery.

The Pleasure That Comes from Pity and Terror

The problem is not to determine whether the expression *pathêmatôn katharsis* can be found elsewhere in Aristotle: for the reasons stated earlier, it cannot. In any case, this would be the wrong approach. The real question is whether or not there are roughly parallel passages, in the *Poetics* or another treatise, that define the effect of tragedy. As it happens, there is just such a passage in Chapter XIV of the *Poetics* itself. It reads:

> Since the poet must arrange the pleasure which comes from pity and terror through imitation, it is clear that this result must be produced by acting upon the incidents.[13]

'Since the poet must arrange the pleasure which comes from pity and terror through imitation' (*tên apo eleou kai phobou dia mimêseôs dei hêdonên paraskeuazein*): in a singular manner, one finds here nearly all the terms that accompanied the mention of catharsis above – pity, terror, imitation, and what imitation must accomplish or realize – but without catharsis itself. In place of catharsis, we find 'pleasure'.

Aristotle states this connection between pleasure and catharsis elsewhere, writing in the *Politics* that sacred chants produce in all those who hear them 'a sort of catharsis and a relief accompanied by pleasure'.[14] There is no contradiction, then, between the mechanism of catharsis and pleasure, as

---

13   Aristotle, *Poetics*, XIV, 1453 b 11–14.
14   Aristotle, *Politics*, VIII, VII, 1342 a 14–15. Translation based on Jean Aubonnet (Paris: Belles Lettres, 1989). As often with Aristotle, the conjunction *kai* (and) does not so much coordinate two different terms as make clear the first by the second, with the sense of '*that is*'. On this, see Jules Tricot, in Aristote, *De l'âme* (Paris: Vrin, 1992) (1st ed., 1934), 2, note 3.

some have erroneously believed.[15] Much to the contrary, the *Politics* confirms the proximity of the two terms, as well as the close parallel between the two passages of the *Poetics*.

While these connections woven between texts do reveal something of the nature of catharsis itself, they seem to complicate the issue of its exact relationship to terror and pity. Indeed, Aristotle never considers terror and pity as enjoyable feelings in and of themselves, but as 'pains' (*lupé*).[16] It is hard to see how unpleasant affects could produce any kind of pleasure. A theory of catharsis must take this difficulty into account.[17]

While the terror/pity pairing is very present in the *Poetics*, Aristotle was not the first to allude to it: it appears earlier in the work of the sophist Gorgias, who includes these emotions among the effects of the oratory art. Plato describes them as the emotions particular to tragedy and, even more specifically, as antithetical emotions.[18] Aristotle draws a similar contrast between terror and pity: too few scholars have noticed it, especially regrettable since this antagonism between the two affects casts light on their relationship with tragic imitation and representation and, as a last resort, with catharsis.

Terror and pity are symmetrical affects in relation to the same event. They diverge according to the point of view from which the event is considered: the same situation will provoke terror in the person experiencing it from the inside

---

15   See Pierre Destrée, 'Éducation morale et *catharsis* tragique', *Études philosophiques*, no. 4 (2003): 534.

16   Aristotle, *Rhetoric*, II, 5, 1382 a 21, and 8, 1385 b 13.

17   Aristotle, *Poetics*, XIII, 1452 b 32–33: 'The arrangement of the most perfect tragedy must . . . imitate actions which excite pity and fear (*phoberôn kai eleeinôn*) (this is in fact the distinctive mark of such an imitation).'

18   Gorgias, *Encomium of Helen*, 82 B 11 (Diels–Kranz 290 18-25); Plato, *Phaedrus*, 268 c. See Raffaele Cantarella, 'Appunti sulla definizione aristotelica della tragedia', *Atti della Accademia nazionale dei Lincei. Rendiconti. Classe di Scienze morali, storiche e filologiche*, no. 30 (1975): 302–5.

and pity in those observing its effects on other people from a distance. Aristotle explains this mechanism twice in the *Rhetoric*. Initially, he uses it to define fear:

> Generally speaking, what is to be feared (*phobera*) are those things that, when they happen to other people or threaten them, can inspire pity in us (*eleeina*).

When he returns to it a second time, it is to take the reversed approach to define pity:

> In a word, we must also admit here that . . . all the things we fear (*phobountai*) for ourselves arouse pity when they happen to others.[19]

Terror and pity are antagonistic emotions, strictly dependent on the subject's position relative to the event. As a general rule, in a real-life situation, where the subject's implication is direct and his position unequivocal, everything is straightforward: we experience either fear or pity, never both at once. The two emotions are mutually exclusive.

Things are very different when it comes to tragedy. Like the art of oratory, tragedy aims to make skilful use of both emotions by setting them off at an accelerated pace. In *Oedipus at Colonus*, Creon's arrival on stage accompanied by an armed escort explicitly aims to arouse terror in the audience. This is equally true of the character's first spoken words, which, through a clever play on the double theatrical address, are directed at both the play's Athenian audience and the old men of Colonus represented by the chorus:

---

19 Aristotle, *Rhetoric*, II, 5, 1382 b 24–26, and 8, 1386 a 27–29. French translation based on Médéric Dufour (1931) (Paris: Belles Lettres, 1991). Quoted by Martha Nussbaum, 'Tragedy and Self-Sufficiency: Plato and Aristotle on Fear and Pity', in *Essays on Aristotle's Poetics*, ed. Amélie Oksenberg Rorty (Princeton, NJ: Princeton University Press, 1992), 274.

'Noble old men, the pride of your land, I seem to catch a terror (*phobon*) in your eyes, a sudden shudder at my arrival.'²⁰ A little later, when Antigone is dragged away from her father, old Oedipus directly refers to himself as an object of pity: 'Ah, woe (*talas*), woe is me!'²¹ Finally, when Polynices finds himself in the position of the supplicant, he expressly appeals to 'Mercy (*Aidôs*) who shares the supreme throne of Zeus'.²² These emotions all come in quick succession, over just a few moments, triggered at speed by the events taking place on stage – in other words, through the art of the playwright who arranged them in this way. The effect is exacerbated by the extreme violence to which the tragic hero's body is generally exposed: Oedipus with his eyes poked out, Philoctetes and his festering wounds, Phaedra's sickly body tormented by passion, old Hecuba's breast ravaged by mourning.

While this intensity of physical violence and acceleration of affects are in and of themselves quite remarkable, the action in tragedy does not stop there. For the events in question are not real: they are, as Aristotle repeats often enough, imitated or represented events. Tragedy offers spectators fictional objects, placed before them to be beheld in the context of a performance; the very word 'theatre' contains an etymological reference to the importance of vision.²³ The emotional reaction caused by imitation – an imitation recognized as such – is not quite of the same nature as the reaction set off by the same event in reality. Unlike in a real situation, the tragic affect can only appear at the end of a complex cognitive process, of which Aristotle indicates the elements at various points in his writings.²⁴

20 Sophocles, *Oedipus at Colonus*, v. 728–730.
21 Ibid., v. 847.
22 Ibid., v. 1267–1268.
23 In the plural, the same word (*theatra*) also allows Aristotle to refer to the audience (*Poetics*, XIII, 1453 a 34).
24 Jonathan Lear rightly emphasizes the difference between emotions brought about by reality and those sparked by imitation ('Katharsis',

When trying to define the type of character who must feature in 'the most beautiful' tragedy, the philosopher makes clear that these should not be

> virtuous men brought from happiness to misfortune (since this is neither pitiful nor terrifying, but is merely repellent). Nor, again, bad men passing from misfortune to happiness (it is the least tragic of all scenarios: indeed it meets none of the conditions; it does not satisfy our humanity [*philantrôpon*] nor is it pitiful or terrifying). Nor should an utter villain fall from happiness to misfortune (a plot of this kind would satisfy our humanity, but it would inspire neither pity nor terror, for pity is aroused by unmerited misfortune and terror by the misfortune of a man like ourselves. Such an event will therefore be neither pitiful nor terrifying).[25]

Given these conditions, Aristotle recommends choosing 'the intermediate case': that of the man who 'is not eminently good and just, yet whose misfortune is brought about not by vice and malice, but by some error or frailty'.[26] And he cites Oedipus as an example. The playwright must choose his characters in a manner suitable to ensure that the audience can identify with the hero, who must be neither totally depraved nor a paragon of virtue, but fit into a relationship of ethical similarity with the spectator. The mechanism of tragic affect can only be properly initiated in the context of an empathic relationship between the audience and what it sees on stage.

In this respect, it is worth noting that the definition of terror seems to have changed between the *Rhetoric* and the *Poetics*: in the former, it refers to a personal misfortune, in the latter, to

Phronesis 33 (1988): 314–26; republished in Rorty, ed., *Essays on Aristotle's Poetics*).

25 Aristotle, *Poetics*, XIII, 1452 b 34–1453 a 7.
26 Ibid., 1453 a 7–10.

that of a 'man like ourselves' (*homoion*). A minimal divergence: it merely reproduces the gap between a real situation and its imitation in tragedy, where the subject's involvement is necessarily indirect. But, according to the Aristotelian theory we have just revisited, what exactly happens in the tragic process? On the one hand, when the hero is unjustly struck by adversity, the audience feels the same emotion towards him as they would in a real situation: pity. On the other, since this is an imitation of reality, the audience also recognizes that the events unfolding on stage have an exemplary value; they can identify with the character; they are witness to the misfortune of a 'man like themselves'. They experience fear.

Two types of fear, to be precise. First, in identifying with a character, the spectator can certainly share the character's fear of the event that threatens him or her: for example, the terror Oedipus and the people of Colonus experience at Creon's arrival. But, on another level, even if the character does not specifically express fear, the spectator can and must experience it: the fear of one day becoming a victim of a misfortune similar to that striking the character. In the *Rhetoric*, Aristotle defines terror as 'a pain and agitation derived from the imagination of a potentially destructive or painful future evil'.[27] When Antigone is torn from her father by Creon and his guards, Oedipus does not express fear, but anger and sorrow, and calls for the pity of those surrounding him. Yet the spectator is nonetheless terrified by the idea of one day being in the same situation as the old blind man. There is never any lack of terror in the audience's experience, precisely because of the empathic force of the good tragic narrative according to Aristotle.[28]

---

27 Aristotle, *Rhetoric*, II, 5, 1382 a 21–22. Translation adapted from *On Rhetoric*, trans. George A. Kennedy (Oxford: Oxford University Press, 2007), 143.

28 See Alexander Nehamas, 'Pity and Fear in the *Rhetoric* and the *Poetics*', in Rorty, *Essays on Aristotle's Poetics*, 303.

The philosopher regards as fundamental this exemplary dimension of events depicted in tragedy and their ability to apply to other individuals than those represented on stage – and in particular to spectators. He even regards it as an essential characteristic of poetry, as opposed to real events such as those described by a historian, for instance. 'Poetry', Aristotle writes, 'is more philosophical and more important than history, for poetry tends to express the general, while history tends to express the particular.'[29]

The consequence of this mechanism of empathy is that the tragedy's audience simultaneously feels terror and pity. Or, more precisely, they initially feel the pity they would normally experience in a real situation. Terror only comes after that, through identification. Conversely, if there is no pity – in other words, according to Aristotle, if the misfortune represented does not appear unjust and undeserved – there is no possibility of fear. Indeed, the spectator – who is generally not a bad person – would not be especially apprehensive about falling victim to a deserved misfortune. A good tragic misfortune must be disproportionate to the error that caused it, as Aristotle suggests in the *Rhetoric*:

> All things to be feared are more fearful when they are due to a mistake that cannot be set right or cannot be remedied because it is impossible in and of itself or because it is not in our power but in the power of our opponents.[30]

Unjust misfortune is therefore a necessary condition, first of pity, then of terror. It is significant that the *Poetics* only ever mentions pity and terror in that order,[31] and not the other

---

29 Aristotle, *Poetics*, IX, 1451 b 5–7.
30 Aristotle, *Rhetoric*, II, 5, 1382 b 21–24.
31 Aristotle, *Poetics*, VI, 1449 b 27; XIII, 1452 a 38, 1453 a 3 and 5; XIV, 1453 b 12. See Cantarella, 'Appunti sulla definizione aristotelica della tragedia', 304.

way around (as preferred by Gorgias), since for the spectator of a tragedy, pity logically precedes fear in the cognitive process. In practice, of course, the two emotions are virtually concurrent. Seeing Creon arrive to take Antigone and Ismene away, we feel pity for Oedipus, from a purely objective point of view. Yet, nearly simultaneously, because Oedipus is 'a man like ourselves' from an ethical perspective, we shudder with empathy, picturing ourselves in his shoes through the effects of subjectivization.

In every case, this concomitance of points of view, characteristic of tragedy, allows pity and terror to be produced if not at the same moment, at least in very quick succession. In the *Poetics*, Aristotle did not randomly choose these two emotions as mere examples of feelings aroused by tragedy: they and they alone are the tragic emotions par excellence, always coupled in the context of theatrical imitation. This is an absolutely essential point to understand the mechanism of catharsis.

The Physiology of Emotions

While we have just confirmed that pity and terror are symmetric emotions on the cognitive level, they are antagonistic on the physiological level. This is very clearly set forth in *Problems*, XXX, 1, which has been confidently attributed to Aristotle himself by numerous philologists following in the footsteps of Cicero, Seneca, Plutarch, Aulus Gellius, and Galen. If it was not written by Aristotle, it is undoubtedly the work of someone in his inner circle.[32]

---

32 On the authenticity of the *Problems* in general and of *Problems*, XXX, 1 in particular, see Hellmut Flashar, in Aristotle, *Problemata physica* (Berlin: Akademie, 1983), 316, 341, 711–17; Pierre Louis, 'Notice', in Aristote, *Problèmes*, vol. 3 (Paris: Belles Lettres, 1994), 23–8. According to Philip J. van der Eijk, even if *Problems*, XXX, 1 were not by Aristotle

In fact, the author's identity is of little importance here. We have seen from Aristotle's approach to catharsis in his own writings that its nature must have been obvious to a reader aware of his ideas: even if *Problems*, XXX, 1 was not written by the philosopher himself, it would still express the way the treatise on *Poetics* was received and understood by his disciples.

This famous problem deals with melancholy – in other words, the influence of black bile (*melaina kholê* or *melagkholia*) on the mind. The Ancients believed that along with blood, yellow bile, and phlegm, black bile was one of the humours of which the mixture (*krasis*) determined not only an individual's physiological state, but also their psychological state. For a Greek person of the fourth century BCE, nothing took place in the mind that did not have a correspondence in the body, and vice versa. The balance of

---

himself, it provides valuable insight into the master's opinions ('Aristotle on Melancholy', in *Medicine and Philosophy in Classical Antiquity: Doctors and Philosophers on Nature, Soul, Health and Disease* [Cambridge: Cambridge University Press, 2005], 139–68). A few previous exegetes have used *Problems*, XXX, 1 to explain tragic catharsis: see Jeanne Croissant, *Aristote et les mystères* (Liège: Faculté de philosophie et lettres, 1932), 63–111; J. Tate, 'Tragedy and the Black Bile', *Hermathena*, no. 50 (1937): 1–25; Hellmut Flashar, 'Die medizinischen Grundlagen der Lehre von der Wirkung der Dichtung in der griechischen Poetik', *Hermes* 84, no. 1 (1956): 12–48. But Croissant and Tate get tangled up in an unlikely homeopathic conception of catharsis (see Aristotle, *Nicomachean Ethics*, II, III, 1104 b 17–18: 'The treatments naturally occur through opposites.') Flashar overly emphasizes the Hippocratic question of humidity. Of all the exegetes, Elizabeth S. Belfiore comes closest to the solution in her remarkable book *Tragic Pleasures: Aristotle on Plot and Emotion* (Princeton, NJ: Princeton University Press, 1992), but she uses *Problems*, I, 42 (308–14), without considering XXX, 1, and devises a complex conceptual construction prompted by cognitivism (catharsis as a process of emotional socialization) that is more an effect of her personal invention than truly rooted in Aristotle. To understand catharsis, we must imperatively return to Aristotle's writings on fear and pity, without overly straying from them as many philosophically inspired readings have a tendency to do. When it comes to this, philology proves to be far more useful than philosophy.

humours and their quality, proportion, and temperature played a primordial part in this system.[33]

Problems, XXX, 1 makes two complementary statements concerning terror and pity. On the one hand, it says that cold makes one fearful:

> The mixture of black bile is sometimes cold like water, sometimes hot, so that when something terrifying (*phoberon*) presents itself, if the mixture is colder, the subject becomes cowardly. For the mixture opens the way to terror, and terror (*phobos*) is cooling.[34]

As we can see, the Aristotelian school posits a complete interaction of the physiological and the psychological, for if the cooling of black bile predisposes to fear, fear itself cools the mixture. But what is true of fear is also true, on the other hand, of pity:

> Wine in large quantities seems to produce the characteristics which we ascribe to the melancholic, and when it is drunk produces a wide variety of feelings, making men ill-tempered, kindly, subject to feelings of pity (*eleêmonas*), and reckless.[35]

Aristotle – or his disciple – adds that this effect of wine, which is due to the heat and breath it naturally contains, is

---

33 This correspondence between mind and body, not to say this materiality of mind and soul, a constant in Hippocratic thought, is found in Aristotle and even, to a certain degree, in Plato. See Philip J. van der Eijk, 'The Matter of Mind: Aristotle on the Biology of "Psychic" Processes and the Bodily Aspects of Thinking', in *Medicine and Philosophy in Classical Antiquity*, 206–38; Jackie Pigeaud, *La Maladie de l'âme: Étude sur la relation de l'âme et du corps dans la tradition médico-philosophique antique* [1981] (Paris: Belles Lettres, 2nd ed., 1989). On the history of the concept of melancholy, see William Marx, *Vie du lettré* (Paris: Minuit, 2009), 101–8.

34 Aristotle, *Problems*, XXX, 1, 954 b 10–13.

35 Ibid., 953 a 33–36.

similar to that of hot black bile.[36] One may easily conclude that a warming of the black bile can produce, like wine, a tendency to pity, among other consequences. Here we see two emotions corresponding to opposite temperatures: the one – terror – is cold, the other – pity – is hot.[37] The cooling black bile causes warming, and vice versa. Conversely, there is no reason to believe that pity warms black bile or that terror cools it. This is clearly the lesson to be drawn from *Problems*, XXX, 1.

It is also a crucially important contribution to the understanding of tragic catharsis, for it brings to light a literally physiological action of tragedy. Or rather a double action, since theatrical representation provokes two contradictory affects, pity and terror, considered to have antagonistic effects: one warms the mixture of black bile, while the other cools it.

What actually is catharsis? The word appears 161 times in Aristotle's body of work. Of these occurrences, 128 – in other words, the vast majority – are found in the biology treatises, while the term is only used five times in the *Politics* and twice in the *Poetics*.[38] This proportion is in and of itself highly significant. Literally, catharsis means *purification*. It could be a religious purification according to the appropriate ritual: this is exactly what is meant the second time the term appears in the *Poetics*. But, most often in Aristotle, the purification is on a physiological level. It is notable, for example, that the word is associated fifty-nine times with menstrual flow. It is associated once with ejaculation.[39]

---

36   Ibid., 953 b 22–24, 954 b 38–39, 955 a 21–22 and 35–36.

37   The Hippocratic corpus also connects terror with cold and pity with heat and humidity (see Flashar, 'Die medizinischen Grundlagen', 30–1).

38   This breakdown is indebted to Belfiore, *Tragic Pleasures*, 292. See also Velvet Yates, 'A Sexual Model of Catharsis', *Apeiron* 31, no. 1 (March 1998): 36.

39   Aristotle, *Problems*, IV, 30, 880 a 32–33. Though this problem may not be by Aristotle himself, the wording is very close to that of XXX, 1, 955 a 23–25.

Catharsis can also refer to a medical *purgation* – though the natural evacuation of excrement or urine without the aid of medication is never referred to.

Many readers of the *Poetics* have been disconcerted by the jumble of physiological and medical meanings of catharsis. Feeling overwhelmed, some have even ironically reported their surprise that the model of menstruation has never been used to explain tragic catharsis (cue bawdy laughter in the gallery).[40] Yet irony is hardly called for: Aristotle and his contemporaries took it for granted that emotions, even when provoked by tragedy, had something to do with physiology and bodily functions. Nothing could be clearer in this regard than the essay *On the Soul*:

> All the passions (*pathê*) of the soul do seem to go in concert with the body: courage, gentleness, fear (*phobos*), pity (*eleos*), audacity, as well as joy and love and hate. For at the same time as them, the body experiences a modification (*paskhei ti*).[41]

Conversely, Aristotle adds, when the body experiences a certain change, the soul can also feel a specific emotion without apparent cause. Anyone who is surprised by this intervention of physiology, who refuses to see it, is condemned to missing the key concerns of the *Poetics*, which are to examine the power of literary forms and their action on readers and spectators. At the end of the day, is it really so surprising that this action is exerted on the body, given that every reader has one?

According to *Problems*, I, 42, which was quite certainly written by Aristotle himself, the purpose of medicine

---

40 Lear, 'Katharsis', 298; quoted by Belfiore, *Tragic Pleasures*, and Yates, 'A Sexual Model', 35, who happily took Lear's joke seriously.

41 Aristotle, *On the Soul*, 403 a 15–19. The argument continues until 403 b 19.

(*pharmakon*) is to 'purify' or 'purge' (*kathairei*), and it is in
its nature to 'cause trouble by an excess of heat or cold'.[42]
This is exactly what pity and terror do by bringing heat to
the mixture of black bile (through pity) at some times and
cold (through terror) at others. Obviously, the effect produced here is not that of a purgation, but rather that of a
purification, comparable to that produced, according to
Problems, V, 40, by walking in freezing air: 'it purifies (*kath-
airousi*) the insides by increasing the heat there.'[43] This
purification takes effect through the contrast between the
heat inside and the cold outside.

For not every purification requires an actual evacuation.
The physiological catharsis aims first to re-establish equilibrium (*katastasis, apokatastasis*) by relieving excesses,
excesses that are not necessarily substances to be evacuated
but sometimes simply degrees of hot and cold. It can also be
both at once: excessive substances *and* temperature. This is
the case with ejaculation, which allows those who have too
much heat to 'relieve themselves (*kouphizontai*) of their sur-
plus (*perittômatos*), namely the excess of breath and heat'.[44]
This is reminiscent of the passage in the *Politics* cited above,
in which 'a sort of catharsis and a relief (*kouphizesthai*)
accompanied by pleasure' are seen as equivalent. Purification is accompanied by relief or alleviation, and it comes
as no surprise that in his treatise *On the Generation of Animals*, Aristotle establishes a certain connection between
catharsis and the sex act.[45]

---

42 Aristotle, *Problems*, I, 42, 864 a 23 and 864 a 10–11. On the
authenticity of this problem, see Louis, 'Notice', in *Problèmes*, vol. 1, 1–8.
43 Aristotle, *Problems*, V, 40, 885 a 25–26.
44 Ibid., XXX, 1, 955 a 25–26.
45 Aristotle, *On the Generation of Animals*, I, 18, 726 a 11–13; IV,
5, 773 b 30–774 a 3.

Solution to the Enigma and Confirmations

The elements are now all in place to allow for an accurate definition of tragic catharsis according to the *Poetics*. It is no more and no less than an action to rebalance the humoral mixture:[46] the pity provoked by tragedy accumulates heat in the mixture of black bile; in return, terror relieves this excess of heat. 'Balance' is the appropriate term, since terror is manifested in exact proportion to the pity that preceded it. This relief through a perpetual alternating movement is what causes pleasure. Pity and terror are not among those 'things that are pleasant by nature'. They become so 'by accident', to use the definitions found in the *Nicomachean Ethics*, where Aristotle defines 'as pleasant by accident those things that are remedial'[47] – in this case, there is indeed a remedy involved, since an equilibrium is restored. This resolves the question of the pleasure caused by affects that are unpleasant in and of themselves.

As we have seen, terror is the emotion specifically tied to representation, since it is determined by the spectator's identification with the characters. Since terror is also the emotion that provokes the final easement in the succession of pity and terror, tragic pleasure is revealed to be a pleasure caused by imitation – and this needed to be demonstrated.

However, one question remains. Given that Aristotle writes that imitation 'uses pity and terror to accomplish the catharsis of such emotions', what exactly are the emotions whose catharsis is accomplished? To date, this problem has

---

46 Taking his cue from Galen, David Samuel Margoliouth also interprets catharsis as a 'restoration of equilibrium', but subsequently adopts a homeopathic approach to the process that lacks clarity ('Introduction', in *The Poetics of Aristotle* [London: Hodder and Stoughton, 1911], 59).

47 Aristotle, *Nicomachean Ethics*, VII, XIV, 7, 1154 b 16–18.

forced every modern exegete without exception to imagine complex conceptual constructions. What is at stake here is the interpretation of *toioutôn*, in *tên tôn toioutôn pathê-matôn katharsin*. Is it 'the catharsis of *these* emotions', in other words of the pity and terror mentioned earlier? Aside from the fact that this is not the exact meaning of *toioutos*, the mechanism in question appears difficult to understand. On the other hand, if it is a matter of the 'catharsis of *such* emotions' or 'emotions *of the same kind*', as the language would tend to indicate, the question of knowing what kind of emotions we are dealing with suddenly opens up before us like an abyss.

To avoid this uncertainty, a minority of interpreters have opted for the translation of *pathêmatôn* as 'events' or 'incidents', which is indeed a possible meaning.[48] But they have merely leaped out of the frying pan and into the fire, for it is exceedingly difficult to understand how imitation could use pity and terror to accomplish the purification of the 'incidents' that take place on stage, without resorting to subtle intellectual adjustments quite remote from Aristotle. The question is not to invent some interpretation of catharsis: the human mind is such that nearly all interpretations are more or less justifiable. The problem is finding the interpretation that is the most congruent with the writings of Aristotle and his school, through the least tortuous means possible.

As it happens, the answer could not be simpler. Once again it can be found in *Problems*, XXX, 1, which classifies affects according to whether they are produced by a warming or a cooling of the mixture of black bile. Among those produced by warming, one finds, in no order, anger, kindness, boldness, elation, euphoria, recklessness, loquacity and sensuality: all emotions or behaviours that pertain to the

---

48   See, for example, Nehamas, 'Pity and Fear', 306–7.

category of pity. In the category of terror, caused by the coldness of the mixture, one finds cowardice, tremulousness, depression, sorrow, stupidity, and taciturnity.[49]

The role of tragic catharsis is therefore to use the alternation of pity and terror to rid the spectator of any correlated emotions, namely those that share pity and terror's association with a change in temperature of black bile: in grammatical terms, the genitive used in the Greek text is called *separative*, as is the case in Aristotle in every other use of the genitive with *katharsis*.[50] One can thus paraphrase the famous passage from the *Poetics* as follows: 'Tragic imitation uses pity and terror to accomplish the purification [of the spectator or reader by delivering him] of emotions of the same kind.'[51]

Such an interpretation of catharsis has the advantage not only of being consistent with Aristotelian theories of the body, but also of resonating with all of the philosopher's moral thinking, which is based on the principle of equilibrium between opposites. 'There are three dispositions', Aristotle writes in the *Nicomachean Ethics*: 'two vices, one of excess, one of deficiency, and only a single virtue, which is in the middle.'[52] Similarly, tragic catharsis consists of reaching a balance between the excessive heat of the mixture of black bile – manifested in the form of pity and associated affects – and the deficiency of this same heat – which corresponds to terror and the other correlated emotions.

---

49   Aristotle, *Problems*, XXX, 1, 953 a 36–954 a 6, 954 a 30–34, 955 a 13–16.

50   Belfiore, *Tragic Pleasures*, 293, has made this point in irrefutable terms.

51   *Toioutôn pathêmatôn* refers either to all the emotions of the same kind as pity and terror, namely those that are associated with a change of temperature of the mixture of black bile; or, respectively, to emotions of the same kind as pity, on the one hand, and on the other, those of the same kind as terror. Concerning the latter case, one finds a similar distributive use of *toioutos* in Plato, *Symposium*, 186 d. Both interpretations amount to the same thing, of course.

52   Aristotle, *Nicomachean Ethics*, II, VIII, 1, 1108 b 11–13. See also *Magna moralia*, I, VIII, 1–2, 1186 a 28–36.

According to Aristotle, the mixture of opposites in such a manner that they moderate each other is a universal principle. It must be sought both in the objects of art and in the body (the two levels are connected since, as we have seen, objects of the senses are held to influence physiological functioning). This is the case with music:

> Everything that is mixed is more pleasant than that which is not, especially in the case of a sensitive object, when the harmonious proportion maintains the power of the two extremes in equal measures.[53]

This mixture is also valid on the moral plane: the ideal for the wise man is not absolute insensitivity (*apatheia*), but a measured use of the affects that allows one affect to be corrected by its opposite.[54] As can be seen, the roots of the theory of tragic catharsis go to the very core of the Aristotelian system.

The rare ancient commentaries on this passage of the *Poetics* made no mistake about it. The venerable Syriac translation already appears to point in this direction, paraphrasing the Aristotelian definition of tragedy as follows: 'Imitation balances the passions by way of pity and fear, and purges those who are passionate.'[55] The idea of equality or balance is crucially important here.

A papyrus found in Herculaneum provides an interesting record of this theory of the moderation of opposites by opposites. In a demonstration apparently intended to illustrate the Aristotelian notion of catharsis, the author states that 'there

---

53 Aristotle, *Problems*, XIX, 38, 921 a 4–6.

54 See Diogenes Laërtius, *Lives and Opinions of Eminent Philosophers*, V, 31. This analysis owes a great deal to Maria Luisa Nardelli, 'La catarsi poetica nel *PHerc.* 1581', *Cronache ercolanesi*, no. 8 (1978): 98.

55 Margoliouth, *The Poetics of Aristotle*, 245 (Latin translation of the Arabic translation of the Syriac translation): 'aequat passiones per misericordiam et metum et purgat illos qui patiuntur.'

is folly in the wisest souls, intemperance in the most moderate; and, similarly, fear in the brave and envy in the magnanimous'.[56] In other words, the mixture of virtues and vices. Or rather, how vices participate in the exercise of virtue.

The philosopher Olympiodorus the Younger recorded another important view of catharsis in his *Commentary on Plato's Alcibiades*:

> Stoic [and Peripatetic] catharsis cures opposites with opposites, applying desire (*epithumian*) to anger (*thumôi*), thus softening the latter, and applying anger to desire, thus strengthening the latter to make it more virile, like when one bends a crooked twig the other way to straighten it, so that the torsion in the opposite direction provides the right balance (*summetron*).

Further down:

> Catharsis cures evil with evil, or at least emotion with emotion.

And finally:

> The Aristotelian form of catharsis cures evil with evil and leads to the right balance (*summetrian*) through the clash of opposites.[57]

---

56 *PHerc.* 1581, fragment II, quoted by Nardelli, 'La catarsi poetica', 100. This may be an excerpt from the Poetics of the epicurean philosopher Philodemus of Gadara (c. 110–c. 35 BCE). The papyrus fragment does not contradict the Aristotelian theory of the happy medium as much as Claudio William Veloso claims ('Aristotle's *Poetics* without Katharsis, Fear, or Pity', *Oxford Studies in Ancient Philosophy* 33 [2007]: 281–2): since a virtue according to Aristotle is the product of two opposite vices, there is indeed a tendency to vice in the most virtuous souls – but it is a tendency impeded by the tendency to the opposite vice.

57 Olympiodore le Jeune (sixth century AD), *Commentaire sur le Premier Alcibiade de Platon*, ed. Leendert Gerrit Westerink (Amsterdam: North-Holland Publishing Company, 1956), 37 (54, 17–22, and 55,

The image of the curved stick you straighten by bending it the other way, a metaphor found earlier in Aristotle,[58] perfectly illustrates the mechanism of tragic catharsis, where pity and terror – and their associated emotions – constantly correct each other in order to achieve a balance.

It follows that catharsis, far from applying only to spectators with an emotional imbalance, is beneficial to all individuals, including the healthiest, because it reinforces or restores their physiological and moral balance: once the humoral balance has been disturbed by one of the two basic tragic emotions, tragic pleasure is found in the correction that the second emotion brings to the operation of the first.

Writing in the *Politics*, Aristotle himself emphasizes the universality of cathartic action. Having noted that listeners to sacred chants are 'restored as if through the action of a cure or a purification (*katharsis*)', he gives a remarkably broad definition of those who benefit from this treatment:

> Exactly this same effect must necessarily be experienced by those people prone to pity or subject to terror and the emotive temperaments in general, but also others, insofar as these emotions can affect every one of them; and all of them experience a kind of purification and a feeling of relief mixed with pleasure.[59]

Over the centuries, many have tried to discredit physiological explanations of catharsis, judging them too heavily

---

12–13) and 94 (146, 2–4). Quoted by Alexandre Nicev, *L'Énigme de la catharsis tragique dans Aristote* (Sofia: Éditions de l'Académie bulgare des sciences, 1970), 183–92. Unfortunately, while his book is rich with information, Nicev mistakenly interprets the mechanism of catharsis as described by Olympiodorus as a homeopathic process. See Belfiore's correction of this error, *Tragic Pleasures*, 328.

58 Aristotle, *Nicomachean Ethics*, II, IX, 4–5, 1109 b 2–8; cited by Belfiore, *Tragic Pleasures*, 329.

59 Aristotle, *Politics*, VIII, VII, 4–5, 1342 a 10–15.

influenced by medicine and claiming that they would restrict the effects of catharsis to people who were sick.[60] Nothing could be further from the truth. On the contrary, in the Aristotelian system, catharsis as a humoral and ethical balancing mechanism proves beneficial to those in good health and also to the wise, to whom it is available as a means to maintain or even improve health and wisdom. With this theory, the philosopher was implicitly responding to the Platonic condemnation of poetry.

This explanation of catharsis has the advantage of being simple and not requiring any concepts other than those employed by Aristotle and his closest disciples. While remaining perfectly consistent with the fundamental principles of Aristotelian ethics, its basis in the complementarity of terror and pity's double nature – as both a cognitive fact and a reality of the humoral system – reconciles the cognitivist reading, favoured by the most recent commentators,[61] with the physiological interpretation of the *Poetics* that imposed itself as the most valid from a philological perspective in the nineteenth century. This double nature is precisely the reason that tragedy can exercise a cathartic function.

If there is a 'purging of the passions', it is not because the terror experienced at the theatre would cure one from real terror (the same goes for pity), but because terror and pity, cold and heat, counteract each other. Unlike the other

---

60 This is the overall criticism levelled at Jacob Bernays's famous thesis, 'Grundzüge der verlorenen Abhandlung des Aristoteles über Wirkung der Tragödie', *Abhandlungen der historischen philologischen Gesellschaft in Breslau* 1 (1857): 135–202.

61 Notable recent cognitivist and emotivist interpretations of catharsis include, along with Belfiore, Lear, Nehamas and Nussbaum in *Essays on Aristotle's Poetics*; Laurent Jenny, 'Poétique et représentation', *Poétique*, no. 58 (April 1984): 171–95; and Sophie Klimis, *Le Statut du mythe dans la Poétique d'Aristote: Les Fondements philosophiques de la tragédie* (Brussels: Ousia, 1997), 129–50.

physiological explanations of catharsis, this one follows an obvious allopathic mechanism,[62] while accounting for tragic pleasure in a way that applies to every kind of spectator, whether ailing or in good health.

A Pre-Kantian Aesthetic

Seen in this light, Aristotelian catharsis has the remarkable particularity of offering a kind of prefiguration of Kantian aesthetics. This may seem paradoxical, as according to Kant the beautiful has all the characteristics of a purposiveness without purpose, detached from practical utility,[63] while Aristotle assigns tragedy a cathartic function beneficial to the spectator's well-being. On the face of it, it seems extremely difficult to join Kantian uselessness with Aristotelian usefulness.

On closer inspection, however, reality proves more complicated. What does tragedy actually do? It has an effect on the humours, warms the mixture of black bile, then cools it, pushing in one direction, then another, in such a manner that it leaves the soul in the state it was in before. The pleasure provided by catharsis is that of an in-between, an equilibrium, a zero-sum game: in short, something that shares a certain quality of fundamental indeterminacy with Kant's idea of the beautiful. Like beauty, catharsis acts without acting. As in a catalytic reaction, which seems not to modify the catalyst, the soul appears to have been left untouched by the cathartic process.

---

62 Regarding this question, see Belfiore, *Tragic Pleasures*, 260–90, who, in agreement with the sixteenth-century humanists Vincenzo Maggi and Antonio Sebastiano Minturno, clearly shows that a homeopathic conception of catharsis is untenable.

63 Immanuel Kant, *Critique of Judgement* [1790], s. 15.

Admittedly, this comparison with Kantian aesthetics should not be pushed too far. In particular, as we have seen, the pleasure provoked by catharsis has far less to do with the beautiful than with the realm of the agreeable – which the German philosopher explicitly contrasts with the beautiful – in that the agreeable is tied to sensations and is based on a 'personal and private feeling', whereas 'the beautiful is that which, apart from concepts, is represented as the object of a universal delight'.[64]

However, unlike Kant's notion of the agreeable, Aristotle's notion of tragic pleasure has a certain universal quality. Every spectator, whether in good health or subject to some humoral pathology, is liable to experience it.[65] Remarkably, Aristotelian catharsis reunites qualities specific to the three terms which Kantian aesthetics attempts to separate: the agreeable, since it provokes pleasure; the good, since it has a medical utility; and the beautiful, since it offers a universal satisfaction and its action is marked by indeterminacy.

Based on this observation, two views suggest themselves. Either we consider Aristotle's reflection as typical of a pre-Kantian state of aesthetic philosophy, and criticize him for having conflated qualities that should on the contrary have been differentiated: the agreeable, the good, and the beautiful. Or, conversely, one might consider that something was lost between Aristotle and Kant, something that enabled a global understanding of the work of art and of the diversity of its action.

---

64 Ibid., s. 6–7. Trans. James Creed Meredith [1952], rev. Nicholas Walker (Oxford: Oxford University Press, 2007).

65 As we have seen, the only spectators seemingly immune to tragic empathy are those who are perfectly virtuous or, on the contrary, excessively malign. Obviously, these cases are rare. But even then, the empathic mechanism of terror and pity would be re-established merely by featuring suitable heroes, as good or as bad as the audience. See Aristotle, *Poetics*, XIII, 1452 b 30–1453 a 12.

That something is obviously the body conceived of as a whole, in which the movements of the soul remain inseparable from those of the humours, and physiology and psychology go hand in hand. The principal difference between the Aristotelian *Poetics* and Kantian aesthetics is that for the first, the operation of tragedy necessarily takes place through the bodily reality of the spectator and reader, while for the second, the effect of art is entirely intellectual and exclusively concerns the realm of ideas and representations.

A Denial of the Body

This radical break between the two aesthetics explains many things and, in particular, the Moderns' difficulty with understanding catharsis. In 1857, when the philologist Jacob Bernays proposed a physiological interpretation of Aristotelian catharsis (for nearly the first time since the Renaissance), he took as his whipping boy an illustrious figure of eighteenth-century aesthetic philosophy, Lessing, whom he accused of having distorted the famous Aristotelian concept in a purely moral direction.[66] Bernays had picked the right target in an intellectual movement which, by denying and misunderstanding the body, had doomed itself to never understand a thing about Aristotle's *Poetics*. The rupture with the aesthetic of the Enlightenment was complete.

---

66 Bernays, 'Grundzüge der verlorenen Abhandlung', 135–9. Bernays was preceded in this endeavour by Henri Weil, 'Über die Wirkung der Tragödie nach Aristoteles', *Verhandlungen der 10. Philologenversammlung*, Basel: 1848, 131–41; reprinted in Matthias Luserke, ed., *Die Aristotelische Katharsis: Dokumente ihrer Deutung im 19. und 20. Jahrhundert* (Hildesheim: Olms, 1991), 69–79. But Bernays's article made the biggest splash. On this subject, see Karlfried Gründer, 'Jacob Bernays und der Streit um die Katharsis' [1968], in Luserke, *Die Aristotelische Katharsis*, 352–85.

Bernays's attack on the intellectualist reading of catharsis would have a lasting impact on the German philological school – and reach far beyond it.[67] But the anti-physiologist reaction did not take long to push back.

Countless moral, aesthetic and intellectual interpretations of catharsis sprang up in the modern era, suggesting that exegetes had nothing more urgent on their agendas than to eliminate everything in Aristotle's writings that involved a physiological mechanism. Extraordinary feats of cunning and imagination were marshalled to erase anything that could remind the tragedy's spectator or reader of organic reality. Countless critics, aiming only to discredit Bernays, described him as the champion of 'a certain medical and psychiatric mechanism specific to the nineteenth century',[68] which they claimed he forcibly applied to Aristotle's text – as if ancient Greece at least as early as Homer had not also believed in the interpenetration of mind and body, and as if the Renaissance humanists, steeped in the ancient texts as they were, had not in turn tended towards a medical conception of catharsis.[69]

---

67 Among the modern physiological interpretations of tragic catharsis, one can mention, aside from those already noted, Ingram Bywater, in Aristotle, *On the Art of Poetry* (Oxford: Clarendon Press, 1909), 152–61; Donald William Lucas, in Aristotle, *Poetics* (Oxford: Clarendon Press, 1968), 273–90; and, especially, Wolfgang Schadewaldt, 'Furcht und Mitleid? Zur Deutung des Aristotelischen Tragödiensatzes', *Hermes* 83, no. 2 (1955): 129–71, which had a significant impact on German philology.

68 Pierre Somville, *Essai sur la Poétique d'Aristote et sur quelques aspects de sa postérité* (Paris: Vrin, 1975), 86. Somville means to reaffirm the 'aesthetic primacy of *Katharsis*' (92). In this intellectualist tradition, though less radical, see the special issue of *Études philosophiques*, no. 4 (2003), introduced by Pierre Destrée, 'La Poétique d'Aristote: Lectures morales et politiques de la tragédie': not one reference to the body.

69 Among the physiological readings of catharsis in the Renaissance, aside from Maggi (1498–1564) and Minturno (1500–1574), who were mentioned earlier, one can note Antonio Scaino (1524–1612). See Abdulla, *Catharsis in Literature*, 17 and 132; Belfiore, *Tragic Pleasures*, 260–90.

Bernays's interpretation is marred by many flaws, which we will return to; it should be corrected and perfected, as I have tried to do here. Yet his fundamental intuition remains correct. While, on the contrary, the history of the reception of the *Poetics* is marked by what must be referred to as a denial of the body.

This denial is so strong that it attempts to strike the litigious words from Aristotle's text: *pathêmatôn katharsin* ('catharsis of the emotions'). Let us be honest: if there were no more catharsis in the *Poetics* than there are polar bears in the Sahara, it would no longer be worth wasting our time on this little scrap of text. That would solve the problem once and for all: no more catharsis, and thus no more body, and every philosophical reading of the *Poetics* going forward could have free rein.

The hypothesis was first put forward in 1912 by the German philologist Heinrich Otte, then picked up and perfected by the Macedonian Mihail D. Petrusevski, before garnering renewed interest in the 2000s.[70] It rests on the fact that Aristotle's text has reached us via a complicated and unreliable tradition. The oldest manuscript of the *Poetics* – the *Parisinus* 1741, dating from the tenth or eleventh century – does not contain the famous term *pathêmatôn katharsin*, but an expression difficult to understand: *mathêmatôn katharsin* ('catharsis of knowledge'). The passage in question was corrupted early on by a scribe's error, or the work of rats and worms.

---

70 See Heinrich Otte, *Kennt Aristoteles die sogennante tragische Katharsis?* (Berlin: Weidmann, 1912); Mihail D. Petrusevski, 'La définition de la tragédie chez Aristote et la catharse', *Annuaire* (Philosophy faculty of Skopje University, History-Philology Section), 1 (1948): 3–17 (summary in French, 6–17); Mihail D. Petrusevski, '*Pathêmatôn katharsin* ou bien *pragmatôn sustasin?*', *Ziva antika / Antiquité vivante* (Skopje), (1954): 209–50 (summary in French, 237–50); Gregory Scott, 'Purging the *Poetics*', *Oxford Studies in Ancient Philosophy* 25 (Winter 2003): 233–63; Veloso, 'Aristotle's Poetics without Katharsis', 255–84.

A correction was in order: a simple change of letter sufficed (*mathêmatôn* altered to *pathêmatôn*). But why not, while we are at it, attempt a more audacious reconstruction, proposing a better conjecture? The most daring hypothesis removes any mention of catharsis, replacing it with an orthographically similar phrase, *pragmatôn sustasin* ('collection of facts'), which is attested to elsewhere in the *Poetics* and provides an acceptable meaning. And this is how 2,000 years of commentary on catharsis suddenly finds itself objectless and disappears down the drain. Brilliant sleight of hand.

Such a solution is lacking neither in elegance nor in panache: Alexander proceeded no differently when he sliced the Gordian knot. Yet it has major drawbacks. On the one hand, it pays no heed to the oldest commentaries on Aristotelian catharsis, notably those in the Herculaneum papyrus or by Olympiodorus the Younger, cited above, but also those by Iambichus and Aristides Quintilianus,[71] which would require dating the scribe's error to a very early point. But, in that case, how can a manuscript independent of the *Parisinus* 1741 – the fourteenth-century *Riccardianus* 46 – contain the *pathêmatôn katharsin* lesson, a lesson itself confirmed by the ancient Syriac and Arabic translations of Aristotle's treatise?[72]

---

71   See August Döring, *Die Kunstlehre des Aristoteles: Ein Beitrag zur Geschichte der Philosophie* (Jena: Dufft, 1876), 332–5.

72   Contrary to what those in favour of cutting the *Poetics* believe, in good philology the fact that a manuscript is more recent does not necessarily make it less reliable: the manuscript's genealogy is more important than its date. The saying goes: *recentiores non deteriores* ('*more recent* does not mean *less good*'). There is no reason, then, to scorn the lessons of the *Riccardianus* 46 on the pretext that it dates from three centuries after the *Parisinus gr.* 1741. On the manuscript tradition of Aristotle's *Poetics* and the independence of the *Parisinus* 1741 and the *Riccardianus* 46, see J. Hardy, 'Introduction', in his 1932 edition and translation, Aristote, *Poétique* (Paris: Belles Lettres, 1990), 22–7; E. Lobel, *The Greek Manuscripts of Aristotle's* Poetics (Oxford: Oxford University Press, 1933); Rudolf Kassel, 'Praefatio' [1965], in Aristotle, *De arte poetica liber* (Oxford: Oxford University Press, 1991), v–xiv.

Additionally, while it is true that the phrase *pathêmatôn katharsin* is a hapax in Greek literature, the same cannot be said of the notion of artistic catharsis, which is found elsewhere in Aristotle. The suppression of the two incriminated words therefore would ultimately necessitate revising not only all the words that surround them, but all the other allusions to musical and tragic catharsis in the *Politics*, which one must admit strips the operation of much of its charm and subtleness: a surgical strike suddenly gives way to carpet bombing.[73]

It should also be noted that such a transformation of the text would only be of interest if the passage were truly incomprehensible and resisted any interpretation, which is assuredly not the case. Consider the critical fortunes of Aristotle's formula: it suffers rather less from an absence than from a plethora of interpretations. And we have just seen that there is a simple and obvious solution to the problem of the 'catharsis of emotions': no reason exists, then, to try to replace the expression by another.

Even if the 'catharsis of emotions' did remain difficult to understand, such a transformation of the text breaks with one of the essential principles of philology: when in doubt, always prefer the most difficult reading or lesson (*lectio difficilior*) to the easiest (*lectio facilior*), because scribes' mistakes tend to be in the latter direction. As it happens, *pragmatôn sustasin* is a *lectio facilior*, since the expression occurs several times in the *Poetics*. The hapax *pathêmatôn katharsin* must therefore be preserved.

Generally speaking, if we were meticulously to examine and modify all the somewhat difficult passages in these ancient texts whose transmission has so often been open to question, there would not be much left of Greek and Latin

---

73 These are the extremes to which Veloso is forced by his initial hypothesis.

literature. The passage in the *Poetics* may well be difficult, but it should be noted that it is not so difficult after making the comparisons I have suggested here with the *Rhetoric*, the *Politics*, and the *Problems*. And there are numerous texts far more complicated than the works of Aristotle – which, thankfully, no one has attempted to tamper with so radically.

Given that Aristotle mentions catharsis in the *Politics*, and other ancient authors also refer to it, it seems that the only reason to go after catharsis, among all other concepts, is because contemporary critics and philosophers are reluctant to accept that tragedy has effects other than an intellectual process. As referred to by catharsis, the body has now become truly inconceivable: there is incredible resistance to the mere idea that it could play a part in tragedy's action on spectators.

Literature and the Body

As it happens, what Aristotle says about tragedy is also applicable to literature in general. As mentioned above, the philosopher was never interested in theatrical performance in and of itself. In his view, everything tragedy does works equally well on a mere reader as on a spectator. The comparison came all the more naturally given that the most frequent ancient practice was not to read in silence, but aloud – or rather to have one's slave read aloud. There was no *reader* in the modern sense of the term: the master was a listener and the slave was a reciter. Which is not so different from theatre.

Moreover, Aristotle certainly lacked knowledge about or even denied the specific nature of theatre as a staged show, partly because of the singular situation of the tragic performance in Athens when he lived there. Such indifference on the part of a thinker of this calibre is regrettable: imagine the reflections on dramatic art Aristotle has deprived us of. But, by way of compensation, this denial of the specificity of theatre vastly expands the scope of the *Poetics*, which is no small thing.

In particular, there are considerable implications to the idea that the catharsis effect can result from a simple reading of the tragic text, unaccompanied by its performance. This means that a piece of literature, in the modern sense of the term, a bare text, could have an effect on the body, could modify it and even – O miracle! – heal it. Today we struggle to associate these properties with the lone idea of literature.

Indeed, does anything today appear more remote from the world, from reality and the body, than literary activity? As defined by the Romantics according to a notion which, in many ways, we still espouse, literature presents itself as the art most qualified to express the intimate movements of the mind, the closest to the pure idea, and the least hindered by the constraints of matter. According to Hegel, it is the art of the intellect par excellence, the last stage before we tip over into the kingdom of ideas, and the ultimate triumph of philosophy.[74]

Aristotle proposes an entirely different view of literature and its powers: his is a literature that penetrates the compound of body and mind and has salutary effects on it through the mechanism of catharsis. Nothing could be more foreign to our modern theory of a language arbitrarily related to reality, stripped of any magic or sacred aura, reduced to a minimal power that linguists since Jakobson have examined under the sober name of *functions*. Similarly, nothing could be more revealing of the gulf that separates our concept of literature from the one that prevailed in

---

74   G. W. F. Hegel, *Aesthetics* (1835), 3rd part, s. 3, ch. III, introduction. See William Marx, *L'Adieu à la littérature: Histoire d'une dévalorisation (XVIIIe–XXe siècle)* (Paris: Minuit, 2005), 52–3.

Aristotle's time, given how radically the very idea of literature has changed over the centuries.

From fourth-century-BCE Athens to the present day,
everything has been transformed an infinite number of times.
Powers, values, references, practices, transmissions, audiences: no aspect of literary activity has remained what it
once was. When reading Homer, Pindar, or the tragedians,
we might think we are dealing with literature, but nothing
could be further from the truth: these texts speak of something else, they *do* something else. Furthermore, they are
barely even texts, in the contemporary sense of the word:
they only appear as such. Ruins or vestiges, rather; that
would be a better term.

How are we to understand the *Poetics*, then? Even the
Rhetorics escape us: the body is infinitely more present there
than we are willing to see. If the body has become inconceivable in tragedy, it is no less so in literature.

Naturally, a handful of writers continued to focus their
efforts on the body. This was still possible before the nineteenth century – readers of *Julie ou la Nouvelle Héloïse*
finished the book in tears, feeling feverish, indisposed,
afflicted with frightful headaches.[75] But today this effect is
only occasional or accidental, for we are constrained by
another concept of literature, by its values and the expectations it is supposed to set up.

The rest are all exceptions. We have Paul Valéry, anchor-
ing his poetics in a theory of the 'nervous system' and stating
that one cannot 'understand poetry' without having 'overcome this prejudice, that must not be excessively old and
pertains to the naïve and not immemorial opposition

---

75 See Raymond Trousson, *Jean-Jacques Rousseau jugé par ses
contemporains* (Paris: Champion, 2000), 210–14 (cited in Marx, *L'Adieu
à la littérature*, 49–50); Alexandre Wenger, *La Fibre littéraire: Le discours
médical sur la lecture au XVIIIe siècle* (Geneva: Droz, 2007).

between the soul and the body'.[76] We have Antonin Artaud, recognizing in Balinese performances 'an idea of theatre [that] has been lost' and defining theatre as one would define 'the plague', that is to say 'a crisis resolved by death or cure'.[77] We have Pierre Guyotat, describing his book *Éden, Éden, Éden* as 'the product of a permanent sexual *desire*, made even more acute over the course of the textual accumulation . . . according to a cyclical, indestructible process' and seeing 'the text' as 'a *confrontation with the language of [his] organic hunger* along a line that it generally follows'.[78] In the same vein, one could also mention Nietzsche, Rimbaud, Whitman and Barthes.

Here and there, the body comes into view on the surface of literature, of *our* literature. It is neither the same body as in Aristotle, nor does it appear on the same terms. Nonetheless, it is a body. Yet these are only surface appearances, with scant consequence for the rest of literary theory and practices, which remain resistant on principle to the slightest intrusion of physiology in their bailiwick.[79] Unless the recent proliferation of such surface appearances signals a turning point, and literature is in the process of redefining itself. Who knows?

---

76 Paul Valéry, *Mélanges* [1939–41], in Œuvres, ed. Jean Hytier [1957–60] (Paris: Gallimard, 1977–80), vol. 1, 335; *Cahiers*, ed. Judith Robinson-Valéry (Paris: Gallimard, 1973–74), vol. 2, 1107 (fragment from 1925–26). Cited by Hugues Marchal, 'Physiologie et théorie littéraire', in *Paul Valéry et l'idée de littérature*, ed. William Marx (2011), fabula.org.

77 Antonin Artaud, *Le Théâtre et son double* [1935], in Œuvres, ed. Évelyne Grossman (Paris: Gallimard, 2004), 555 and 521. English translation: *The Theatre and Its Double*, trans. Mary Caroline Richards (New York: Grove Press, 1958), 31.

78 Pierre Guyotat, *Littérature interdite* (Paris: Gallimard, 1972), 68–9. The italics are Guyotat's.

79 Perhaps this is how one should consider the challenge to the physiological interpretation of catharsis by Jon-Arild Olsen, ' "En cette affliction consiste son Plaisir": Sur le paradoxe du Plaisir tragique', *Poétique*, no. 137 (February 2004): 3–17.

Freud and Catharsis

The fact remains that the only truly consistent link between language and the body to have appeared since Romanticism, as well as the only clear assertion of the former's effects on the latter, are found, not in actual literature – hardly a surprise, given that literature established itself precisely by driving organic reality as far away as possible – but in the newly created science of psychoanalysis. Could it be a coincidence, then, that this new science does not lead us very far from Aristotle and tragedy? For the *Poetics* and psychoanalysis are like kin – biological and by marriage, indeed, for it so happens that Sigmund Freud was married to Jacob Bernays's niece, Martha. The great philologist who brought the physiological interpretation of catharsis back to the fore and the creator of a treatment for maladies of the soul and body through talking were connected not only by obvious intellectual affinities, but by a real family relationship.

It is highly plausible that Freud knew of the famous theory of his uncle by marriage, though he did not meet Martha until after the philologist's death. In 1932, he sent Arnold Zweig a copy of a recent book on Bernays and recommended that he read it.[80] However, Freud's encounter with the great Hellenist's work went much further back, to his first years of practice as a young doctor, when he was working in

---

80 This was an edition of Bernays's correspondence, *Ein Lebensbild in Briefen*, ed. Michael Fraenkel (Breslau: Marcus, 1932). See Hermann Funke, 'Bernays und die aristotelische Poetik', in *Jacob Bernays: Un philologue juif*, ed. John Glicker and André Laks, vol. 16 of *Cahiers de philologie* (Villeneuve-d'Ascq: Presses Universitaires du Septentrion, 1996), 74. For an overview of the relationship between Freud and Bernays, see Gründer, 'Jacob Bernays', 373–6; Funke, 'Bernays und die aristotelische Poetik', 70–5; Abdulla, *Catharsis in Literature*, 26–44 (on catharsis in Freud and other psychoanalysts). For a distinctly more philosophical approach, see Jonathan Lear, *Love and Its Place in Nature* (New York: Farrar, Straus & Giroux, 1990), 29–69.

association with his colleague Josef Breuer and there was no talk yet of psychoanalysis, but of the 'cathartic method'. Later, Freud would assert his divergence from Breuer by giving up hypnosis, which was an integral part of the 'cathartic' treatment, and calling his own method 'analytical'.[81] Nonetheless, Freud's contemporaries were not misled. They saw the parallel between Aristotle's notion of tragic catharsis and these new therapeutic methods that worked like tragedy in providing 'deliverance' from or 'discharge' of (*Entladung*) previously repressed, painful affects: this was catharsis as purgation, just as Bernays suggested.[82]

In fact, the real Aristotelian catharsis must be understood less as a purgation than as a purification and a balancing of the humours: strictly speaking, the idea of 'discharge' is foreign to the definition of catharsis found in the *Poetics*. And this is why Bernays appears as the necessary link between Aristotle's *Poetics* and Freud and Breuer's analytical or cathartic treatment.

Yet this is not the essential point of intersection between the Viennese psychoanalyst and the Philosopher of Stagira. By borrowing from Bernays the image of purgation – which is in fact foreign to the *Poetics* – Freud also lays claim to a principle that is, on the contrary, the very foundation of

---

81 Sigmund Freud, *On Psychotherapy* [*Über Psychotherapie*, 1905], in *The Standard Edition of the Complete Psychological Works of Sigmund Freud*, translated from the German under the general editorship of James Strachey, in collaboration with Anna Freud, assisted by Alix Strachey and Alan Tyson (London: Hogarth Press, 1953–74), vol. 7, 259; *An Autobiographical Study* [*Selbstdarstellung*, 1925], ibid., vol. 10, 19–28.

82 See Alfred von Berger, 'Wahrheit und Irrtum in der Katharsistheorie des Aristoteles', in *Aristote, Poetik*, ed. and trans. Theodor Gomperz (Leipzig: Veit, 1897), 69–98; reprinted in Luserke, *Aristotelische Katharsis*, 128–56 (in particular 139–47). Cited by Gründer, 'Jacob Bernays', 374. See also the commentary on Berger's article by Johannes Volkelt, 'Die tragische Entladung der Affekte' [1898] in Luserke, 157–72. Bernays uses the term *Entladung* to translate *katharsin*, 'Grundzüge', 148.

tragic catharsis in Aristotle: the idea, simply, that language, words, or a text can have a direct impact on the functioning of the body; that they can improve a person's well-being, or even effect a cure. Thus was restored a faculty that had been banished from modern literature, but it was restored elsewhere than in literature, of course: in a new discipline that claimed to explore parts of the human mind still unknown. Now the lost link between the body and language was recreated, and some of literature's most immemorial powers switched camps.

From this perspective, and despite the name change, Freud deepened the relationship with Aristotle by giving up the 'cathartic' treatment for psychoanalysis itself. The shelving of hypnosis as a method reinforced the purely verbal aspect of the analytical treatment: from that point on, the use of language was considered sufficient to treat patients and to allow them to recover repressed memories and desires. Just as in the *Poetics* Aristotle saw the power of tragedy exclusively concentrated in its textual existence, so psychoanalysis turned to pure language to become more effective. The subsequent development of psychoanalytic theory's linguistic dimension by Jacques Lacan would merely push through to its conclusion and outer limit an evolution initiated by Freud – but already perceptible in Aristotle.

Psychoanalysis was born in part of an attempt to explain the power of tragedy: the confrontation with the Greek philosopher remains extremely direct here. In an outline for a 1905 article on 'psychopathic characters on the stage' – which opens, of course, with a reference to the *Poetics* – Freud formulates the theory that only a neurotic can derive pleasure from the spectacle of a hero who is himself neurotic.[83]

---

83   The article was only published posthumously: Freud, 'Psychopathic Characters on the Stage' ('Psychopathische Personen auf der Bühne', 1905–06, 1st ed. 1942), in *The Standard Edition*, vol. 7, 308–9.

This seems to be exactly what Bernays was saying when he stated that according to Aristotle only sick temperaments, subject to passions (*pathêtikoi*), would be liable to benefit from catharsis and therefore to derive pleasure from tragedy.[84] In this regard, Bernays was mistaken: he has rightfully been taken to task for it. It is nonetheless singular that Freud tried to demonstrate a theory similar to that of the great philologist.

In 1905, Freud's model was *Hamlet*, presented as the modern drama par excellence; in 1917, Greek tragedy was used as an example in his *Introductory Lectures on Psychoanalysis* – above all, *Oedipus Rex*. This was not by chance. Twenty years earlier, the theory of the Oedipus complex as described in a letter to Wilhelm Fliess was directly inspired by questions about Sophocles's play.[85] The key issue was to explain why we consent to see events represented on stage which ought surely to outrage us. Freud's theory was that, without knowing it, we recognize in tragedy a 'psychological truth'. The spectator accepts the condemnation of Oedipus because he feels within himself an indistinct but profound guilt:

> He reacts as though by self-analysis he had recognized the Oedipus complex in himself and had unveiled the will of the gods and the oracles as exalted disguises of his own unconscious. It is as though he was obliged to remember the two wishes – to do away with his father and in place of him to take his mother to wife – and to be horrified at them. And he understands the dramatist's voice as though it were saying to him: 'You are struggling in vain against your responsibility and are protesting in vain of what you have done in

---

84 Bernays, 'Grundzüge', 149.
85 Sigmund Freud, *The Complete Letters of Sigmund Freud to Wilhelm Fliess, 1887–1904*, ed. Jeffrey Moussaief Masson (Cambridge, MA: Belknap Press, 1985), 270–3 (letter dated 15 October 1897).

opposition to these criminal intentions. You are guilty, for you have not been able to destroy them; they still persist in you unconsciously.'[86]

The tragedy functions as an analytical treatment by bringing repressed feelings and desires to a preconscious state. Or, to put it more precisely, the treatment invented by Freud follows the model of tragedy: is not the idea of the Oedipus complex directly inspired by Sophocles having Jocasta say that 'many a mortal has shared his mother's bed in his dreams'?[87]

As Pierre Bayard accurately points out, Freud does not naïvely apply psychoanalysis to literature. He does the exact opposite: he imports concepts, experiences, and properties he found in reading the Greek tragedians to his medical practice.[88] Psychoanalysis was born at the precise moment when a Viennese doctor decided to deploy in his own therapy the power over the body that Aristotle attributed to tragedy.

For the Greek philosopher, tragic catharsis and sexual pleasure had the same structure: ejaculation, in particular, is closely related to the purgation of an excess and restoring the humours to equilibrium.[89] As Freud sees it, the relationship between these two pleasures is instead located in the realm of phantasy: *Oedipus Rex* offers to the unconscious the staged representation of an infantile desire. But, in both cases, the idea is indeed that there is a common model to both pleasures, and that tragedy is a form of treatment.

---

86 Sigmund Freud, *Introductory Lectures on Psycho-Analysis* (*Vorlesungen zur Einführung in die Psychoanalyse*, 1917) in *The Standard Edition*, vol. 16, 264.

87 Sophocles, *Oedipus Rex*, v. 981–982. Plato reiterates the same idea in *The Republic*, IX, 571 c–d.

88 Pierre Bayard, *Peut-on appliquer la littérature à la psychanalyse?* (Paris: Minuit, 2004), 25.

89 Aristotle, *Problems*, XXX, I, 955 a 23–25. See Yates, 'A Sexual Model', 35–57.

One could carry the parallels between the two theories further. In the same way that, according to Aristotle, a catharsis occurs in all spectators, whether ill or healthy – since all of them experience terror or pity – the success of *Oedipus Rex* is, for Freud, as universal as the complex it reveals, since the play sets off in all spectators both horror and the diffuse recognition of a hidden, ancient desire. In the same way that Aristotle sees terror and pity as offsetting each other, Freud considers tragedy's ultimate value to be the conjunction of a recognition of self and a distancing: the spectator simultaneously moves towards the hero and steps back. The greater the horror, the more deeply desire is repressed. Terror and pity, repulsion and desire: the psychoanalyst and Aristotle agree that tragedy's effectiveness depends on a pair of antagonistic feelings, the simultaneous action of which causes the treatment, whether it be cathartic or analytical.

That Sophocles was perfectly aware of this is shown when he has the old men of Colonus tell Oedipus: 'It is *terrible* to awaken long-sleeping evil, stranger. Nevertheless, I *long* to hear.'[90] This opposition between the contradictory movements of horror and attraction is a significant part of the tragic mechanism, the very mechanism that according to German philosophy forces events to follow a certain course, however much it may be feared, as if they were driven by an inexorable fate.[91] From fate to desire, the distance is not so great: 'Time is a child at play, moving the pawns: royalty of a child',[92] wrote Heraclitus, reducing the course of history to the simple fulfilment of a child's whim – or else to an infantile desire, which leads Oedipus unwittingly to kill his father and marry his mother.

---

90 Sophocles, *Oedipus at Colonus*, v. 510–512. English translation from Belfiore, *Tragic Pleasures*, 344. My emphasis.

91 See Chapter 2.

92 Heraclitus, fr. B 52, French translation after Marcel Conche [1986] (Paris: Presses Universitaires de France, 1998), 446.

Modern philosophers believed that what they saw in this tragedy was the body of the hero condemned by tragic pressure to do what he does not want to do. On the contrary, Aristotle finds in tragedy a beneficial action on another body: that of the reader and the spectator. Twentieth-century criticism readily picked up this concept of catharsis and adapted it at every opportunity – but always left out the body.[93] Literature no longer wanted this power attributed by the Ancients to tragedy and language, so who could blame Freud for claiming it? What doctor would deign to prescribe her patients a play by Sophocles? And yet, why not? For too long, we forgot that in Antiquity reading out loud was prescribed by doctors as a fully fledged therapeutic act.[94] It is just up to us – readers, critics, writers – to follow suit and accept this power of tragedy as a gift that Aristotle made to literature.

93 This hijacking of catharsis was particularly prevalent in formalist-inspired criticism and the New Criticism. See Abdulla, *Catharsis in Literature*.

94 See Heinrich von Staden, 'La lecture comme thérapie dans la médecine gréco-romaine', in *Comptes rendus des séances de l'année – Académie des inscriptions et belles-lettres*, 146th year, no. 2 (2002): 803–22. Nonetheless, this treatment did not have the cognitive dimension that Aristotle identifies in catharsis.

Sixth Episode and Exodos

Death and Transfiguration

Suddenly, lightning streaks the sky amid horrifying peals of thunder: unquestionable manifestations of Zeus. Oedipus senses that his end is near. He orders his two daughters to follow him, along with Theseus, who has hurried back: without a guide and without support, the blind man will lead them to the place where his life must end. His tomb will benefit the city of Athens, on condition that the king only reveal its location to his successor, and so on for generations to come; even Ismene and Antigone will be kept in the dark. All exit behind Oedipus.

A messenger soon returns to the citizens of Colonus, who have remained alone on stage, and describes the hero's last moments. The old man finally came to a halt close to a chasm, equidistant from the rock of Thorikos, the hollow pear tree, the stone tomb, and the crater where Theseus and Pirithous once made a pledge to each other before descending into the underworld. As soon as his daughters had stripped him of his rags, washed him with fresh water and dressed him in the ritual garments, the sky and earth rumbled again: time was of the essence. As the father embraced his children and spoke his last words to them, a voice rang out from all sides. It was a god, calling insistently: 'You, you there, Oedipus – what are we waiting for? You have dawdled too long.' After asking Theseus to take care of his daughters, the old man sent Antigone and Ismene away with the rest of the procession: the king of Athens alone would be allowed to witness the miracle brewing. The procession moved away, only to turn back a few moments later: Oedipus had disappeared and Theseus covered his eyes as if before an unbearable vision, then prostrated himself and stood up again, adoring in a single movement the earth and the sky, the dwelling of the gods. How did the other man vanish? Was he carried to Olympus or engulfed in the abyss? No one knew. This brings the messenger's narrative to an end.

Weeping is heard: Antigone and Ismene bewail the death of their father. To make their misfortune worse, there is no grave over which to carry out the funeral rites. Theseus interrupts their mourning song: no mortal can approach the sacred tomb. This being so, Antigone wants at least to return to Thebes to prevent her two brothers from killing each other. The king of Athens promises to help her to do so, and the tragedy ends.[1]

---

1 *Exodos* is the moment when the chorus exits the stage.

4

The God

*In memoriam Karl Otfried Müller (1797–1840)
and Charles Lenormant (1802–1859)*

The denouement of *Oedipus at Colonus* is one of the most striking passages in ancient literature. Wonders come in rapid succession: rolls of thunder, lightning in the sky, rumbling from the ground, sight suddenly returned to a blind man, funeral rites carried out for a living person, disembodied voices in the air, an unexplained disappearance and horrifying apparitions, a forbidden tomb and impossible mourning. The powers of the underworld and those above are combined in a single adoration. The way of the world is broken. The supernatural rules.

Yet these events are as concealed from view as the grave of the former king of Thebes: most happen far from the stage and are only revealed to the audience by a messenger. The audience's frustration exactly matches that of Antigone and Ismene as they are prevented from accessing the tomb, and the mystery remains total: no one will learn what really happened, which god intervened, and what fate Oedipus met with and why. We have now reached the brink of the unspeakable and the invisible. We are struck with the astonishment that the initiates of Eleusis must have felt, *mutatis mutandis*, when they were shown the contents of the enigmatic basket. Will we have to follow their example and keep our mouths shut?

From this point on, one can only speak by analogy, and these analogies flood the mind of the contemporary reader or spectator familiar with Judeo-Christian culture. The call of the god is like Moses's and Samuel's vocation, or the voice that resounds from the sky during Jesus's baptism; the prohibition on seeing Oedipus disappear recalls Lot and his family being forbidden to witness the destruction of Sodom; Theseus covering his eyes is Moses hiding his face before the burning bush, or the shiver of horror that rattles Job's friend Eliphaz when he is faced with God's envoy.[1]

Comparisons are imperfect, of course. In a context such as this, references to the Bible must be handled with the utmost caution. Yet both the denouement of *Oedipus at Colonus* and the Bible feature the intervention of a transcendent force that defies all expectations. Is it really so strange that human reactions to this epiphany should be similar on both sides of the Mediterranean? The Ancients themselves would hardly have been surprised by this similarity, because they were used to the gods' propensity to change names from one city-state to another. Does it fall to us to approach this matter with more delicacy than they displayed with regard to their own divinities?

Before setting out to consider tragedy's religious value, the reader must be warned: this entire chapter will be full of scruples. The scruples of all the scholars who for two centuries have attempted to clear this matter up. The scruples of the believer before coming to the altar and participating in the sacrifice. For one can only tremble upon touching these objects. Do not expect to find absolute truth in these pages, other than beneath the veil of aporia. This is the only way to approach the god.

---

1 See, respectively, Exodus III, 4; 1 Samuel III, 4–18; Matthew III, 17; Genesis XIX, 17–26; Exodus III, 6; Job IV, 14–15. The last reference is found in Richard Claverhouse Jebb's edition of Sophocles, *The Plays and Fragments, II: The Oedipus Coloneus* (Cambridge: Cambridge University Press, 1889 [1st ed., 1886]), 252, note to v. 1651.

Tragedy Reduced to Pure Reason

It is a critical commonplace to compare Sophocles's last tragedy with biblical revelation and Christianity. Hegel was not the first to attempt it. In his *Lectures on Aesthetics*, the German philosopher compares Oedipus being expelled from Thebes to Adam and Eve being banished from earthly paradise, then pushes the parallel a little further:

> And yet this sorely afflicted man who in Colonus instead of granting his son's plea for his return, dispatched him his own Erinys, he who expunges all his own inner discord and purifies himself within, is called by a god to him; his blind eye clears (*verklärt*) and lights up; his bones become the salvation and treasure of the city-state that gave him its hospitality. This transfiguration (*Verklärung*) in death is the best manifestation of his reconciliation – and our own – within his own self and personality. Attempts have been made to find a Christian tone in this vision of a sinner whom God welcomes in his grace and in this fate that escapes finiteness and which bliss redeems in death. However, the Christian religion's reconciliation is a trans-figuration of the soul which, bathed in the spring of eternal salvation, is lifted above its reality and its actions, turning the heart itself into the tomb of the heart – for such is the power of the spirit – and settling the accusations linked to its earthly trans-gressions by abandoning its own earthly individuality and now holding itself secure against those accusations in the cer-tainty of a purely spiritual eternal bliss. Oedipus's transfigu-ration, on the contrary, is still only that ancient production of consciousness, created from the conflict of moral powers and the offences to unity and harmony of the *moral* content itself.[2]

---

2   G. W. F. Hegel, *Vorlesungen über die Ästhetik*, ed. Heinrich Gustav Hotho [1838], vol. 3, in *Sämtliche Werke*, ed. Hermann Glockner

THE TOMB OF OEDIPUS

Hegel's beautiful meditation locates *Oedipus at Colonus* in a history of the human spirit discovering salvation. It seeks to pinpoint the play's rightful place between a pagan, archaic conception of transgression and the specifically Christian idea of redemption. In so doing, Hegel explicitly goes against the many earlier thinkers who saw in it a prefiguration of Christian salvation.

It is difficult today not to subscribe to a programme so careful to avoid historical confusion and dubious syncretism. Yet we lose something of *Oedipus at Colonus* in this laudable effort – and not just of *Oedipus*, but of all of Greek tragedy. By rejecting a Christian interpretation of the play, Hegel is also led to repudiate any religious reading of the work: in other words, he throws the baby out with the baptism water. According to the philosopher, Oedipus's salvation, if salvation there is, is simply the manifestation of a rationality and morality that have been reconciled with themselves. Reason and consciousness are the only agents of this miraculous outcome. It would seem that there is no room for the god's intervention at this unique moment in the evolution of the mind, in which Logos advances to the level of an absolute: in Athens, the triumph of Sophocles's last play coincided with the peak of Socrates's influence.

As seductive as it may be from the perspective of a phenomenology of the mind, this reduction of tragedy to pure reason also breaks with everything we know about the

---

(Stuttgart: Frommann, 1964, reissue of the 4th ed.), 558. English translation based on Hegel, *Aesthetics: Lectures on Fine Art*, vol. 2, trans. T. M. Knox (Oxford: Clarendon Press, 1975), 1219–20. Hegel expresses similar ideas and formulations on *Oedipus at Colonus* in *Vorlesungen über die Philosophie der Religion*, second part, ed. Philipp Marheineke (Berlin, 2nd ed., 1840), 135–6, 156 (1827 text); and in *Vorlesungen über die Philosophie der Religion, Teil 2: Die Bestimmte Religion*, ed. Walter Jaeschke, in *Vorlesungen: Ausgewählte Nachschriften und Manuskripte*, vol. 4 (Hamburg: Meiner, 1985), 396 (1824 text). In substance, Hegel's position in his lectures varied far less than is claimed by Lowell Edmunds, *Oedipus* (New York: Routledge, 2006), 104.

religious dimension of these performances – and far more is unknown to us than known. These are contradictions of which scholars have been fully aware: a significant part of nineteenth-century philology was specifically devoted to overcoming or circumventing the Hegelian theory that the tragic is one of the most perfect expressions of triumphant rationality and morality, without ever contradicting it outright. As we saw above, this endeavour culminated with Wilamowitz's work on tragedy.[3] But attacks came fast and furious long before the great German philologist joined the fray.

Two Tombs at Colonus

A present-day traveller to Athens who climbed to the top of the hillock of Colonus, now a public park, would find an open-air theatre and a playground, next to which stand two stelae encircled by a railing. One is in the shape of an ancient ewer and contains the heart of a French archaeologist who died in Athens in 1859: Charles Lenormant, director of the Cabinet des Médailles at the Bibliothèque Nationale, a professor at the Collège de France, and a member of the Académie des Inscriptions et Belles-Lettres.[4] The other marks the grave of one of Lenormant's most famous colleagues, Karl Otfried Müller, a professor at the University of Göttingen, who died of sunstroke nineteen years before him, after conducting excavations on the site of Delphi.

Nothing predisposed these two scholars to cohabitate in death. Lenormant was a Catholic conservative, who came late to Greek and accompanied Champollion on his big

---

3 See Chapter 2, 'The Idea'.
4 It appears that the urn was replaced by a copy in 1936, but it is not clear what happened to Lenormant's heart in the process.

THE TOMB OF OEDIPUS

expedition to Egypt. Like his French colleagues, he was quite suspicious of Germanic philology. Müller was a staunch liberal, a declared opponent to the authoritarian reign of King Ernest Augustus I of Hanover and the most inspired disciple of August Böckh, who would revolutionize ancient studies as the founder of the 'philology of things' (*Sachphilologie*) – as opposed to philology purely devoted to words (*Wortphilologie*).

Nothing predisposed these two men to cohabitate in death other than Oedipus himself, who was not averse to offering them his funerary hospitality somewhere in the vicinity of his own grave, as if wishing to thank them for having referred to Sophocles's last play in their writings, however marginally: gods and heroes sometimes express a fatal gratitude. However, this gratitude was well deserved, for both scholars sought to emphasize the religious and anthropological dimension of tragedy, ignoring the rationalist reduction proposed by Hegel.

Müller's commentary on *The Eumenides* includes some reflections on the role of the Erinys in *Oedipus at Colonus*: if the hero kills his father at the intersection of several roads, and if he dies halfway between Theseus and Pirithous's crater, Thorikos's rock, the hollow pear tree, and the stone tomb, it is because the Erinys set up their homes at crossroads. Oedipus's whole life is governed by the confrontation with these goddesses, until he comes into their good graces:

> In sublime peace and enthusiasm, he impatiently goes to meet an expected death in order to bring, like a demon in his occult action, eternal salvation to the land where he himself was granted peace and reconciliation with the Erinys. Therefore, this tragedy is the triumph of distress and suffering over man's powers and presumption, the metamorphosis into a divine sublimity of what seemed according to human

conceptions to be no more than sadness and lamentation, a
mystical transfiguration of death.[5]

This marks a return to the 'transfiguration' described by
Hegel, only this time inserted once more into the context
of paganism. Oedipus is transformed, not into an allegory of
victorious reason or morals nor into a precursor of Christ,
but into a 'demon' (*daimôn*), one of those beings who popul-
ate the Greek cosmos as intermediaries between the gods
and man. Müller's mysticism has nothing to do with some
kind of progress in moral consciousness: it is entirely rooted
in the cultural reality of ancient Greece.

Oedipus in Orléans

A few years later, Charles Lenormant would relate all the
mysteries of *Oedipus at Colonus* to this same pagan religion.
The opportunity came to him via an apparently inconsequential event: on 29 July 1857, the students of the minor
seminary of Orléans gave a performance of Sophocles's play
in ancient Greek. They were not new to Sophocles: two years
earlier, they had staged *Philoctetes*. This time, the seminary's
management wanted to give the performance a society
veneer. *Le Moniteur du Loiret*, the local paper, proudly
described the prestigious audience:

> In the first row, next to His Grace the Bishop of Orléans, one
> could recognize His Grace the Archbishop of Tours presiding
> over the performance. – Among the eminent literary figures,
> one could see M. Villemain, M. Saint-Marc Girardin, M.

---

5 Karl Otfried Müller, 'Über den Inhalt und die Composition der
Eumeniden', in Aeschylus, *Eumeniden*, ed. K. O. Müller, (Göttingen:
Dieterich, 1833), 172–3.

Patin, members of the Académie Française; M. Hase, M. Lenormant, M. Régnier of the Académie des Inscriptions et Belles-Lettres; M. Ingres of the Académie des Beaux-Arts, who had come to admire one of the works of that Antiquity which has so often and so happily inspired his brush. There were therefore eight members of the Institute honouring and encouraging this celebration of classical studies with their presence.[6]

Eight, because the Bishop of Orléans, His Grace Félix Dupanloup, was also a member of the Académie Française. We'll skip the rest of the description, including the long list of local notables. That an end-of-year school show should command such a distinguished turnout is evidence of the degree to which the school was then respected.

But this event was only inconsequential in appearance, for it played a part in the perpetual struggle between public and Catholic education – the latter having recently won a privileged position thanks to the Falloux Laws. In particular, the performance contributed to the great controversy over the reforms passed by minister of public education Hippolyte Fortoul, which instituted a 'bifurcation' between the literary and scientific baccalaureates, thereby limiting the place of classical studies.[7] In this context, the Catholic church sought to impose itself as the last bastion of an endangered field of knowledge. The diocese of Orléans, under the leadership of its flamboyant bishop, was not alone in throwing its hat into the ring: the minor seminary of Paris had organized a

---

6 A. [Abel?] Quinton, 'Représentation d'*Œdipe à Colone*', *Le Moniteur du Loiret*, 30 or 31 July 1857; reissued in *Souvenir de la représentation d'Œdipe à Colone par les élèves du petit séminaire d'Orléans, 29 juillet, 1857* (Orléans: Pesty, 1857), 12.

7 Primarily enacted through the decree of 10 April 1852 and the ministerial instructions of 15 November 1854. See Maurice Gontard, 'Une réforme de l'enseignement secondaire au XIXe siècle: "La bifurcation" (1852–1865)', *Revue française de pédagogie* 20, no. 1 (1972): 6–14.

similar performance of ancient theatre a few days earlier, with a staging of Aristophanes's *Plutus*.[8]

In other words, many audience members did not show up on 29 July 1857 merely to applaud third-year students treading the boards, but to take sides in a controversy then burning through French society. This was precisely the spirit in which Charles Lenormant came to Orléans: 'Despite the hindrances of the baccalaureate,' he wrote, 'it is only in ecclesiastical institutions that people have remained faithful to tradition.'[9] And he prided himself on it.

Yet, contrary to all expectations, while the archaeologist generously praised the performance in his review in *Le Correspondant*, the organ of the Catholic opposition to the Second Empire, he nonetheless expressed serious reservations about the entire enterprise. Not because of the predictable awkwardness of the young actors, the anachronism of Mendelssohn's music,[10] or other historical inaccuracies of production (the chlamyses fastened '*on both shoulders* so the actors don't lose them by gesticulating', the grotesquely incorrect pronunciation);[11] on the whole, none of this detracted from the performance's naïve charm. Instead, his objection concerned the very principle of the performance and the choice of the play. Was *Oedipus at Colonus* really the work best suited to demonstrate the value of classical studies for the intellectual, moral, and religious formation of a young nineteenth-century man?

The answer was obvious to the students' Greek master and organizer of these theatrical festivities: as he saw it, the continuity between *Oedipus at Colonus* and the teachings of

---

8 See Charles Lenormant, '*Œdipe à Colone* au petit séminaire d'Orléans', *Le Correspondant* 41 (1857): 681.

9 Ibid.

10 Felix Mendelssohn Bartholdy had composed stage music for *Oedipus at Colonus* in 1845.

11 Lenormant, '*Œdipe à Colone*', 680 and 710–12. His italics.

Christianity was clear. The minor seminar professor was not alone in thinking so, as he could amply demonstrate by quoting the great Saint-Marc Girardin's *Cours de littérature dramatique* (*Lessons on Dramatic Literature*): 'Everything in Oedipus calls to mind "the idea of the sanctity of paternal rights".' The play allows one 'to verify the divine words spoken on Mount Sinai: "*Honour your father and mother, so that you may live long in the land the Lord your God is giving you.*" (M. Saint-Marc Girardin) Such is the religious magnitude of Sophocles's drama.'

There was also Joseph de Maistre, who echoed the church fathers in calling the pagan writers 'the Human Prelude to the Gospel'. Or Father Eugène Pion de Hersant, who was full of enthusiasm in describing Sophocles's masterpiece:

> It is the work of an old man who had not yet been enlightened by the lights of Christianity, but who had collected over his long life, in the company of wise men, in the experience of his misfortunes, in the profound meditations of his genius, the scattered lights of the primitive traditions . . . It takes little more than a few words to disperse the cloud of ancient fatalism, and reveal a glimpse of the divine features of Providence.[12]

In staging *Oedipus at Colonus*, these third-year students were practically diving straight into the mysteries of Christian revelation. This naïve biblification and Christianization

---

12 [Eugène Pion de Hersant], 'Préface', in Sophocle, *Œdipe à Colone*, ed. E. Pion de Hersant (Orléans: Pesty, 1857), iii–viii; reissued in *Souvenir de la représentation d'Œdipe à Colone*, 7, 9–10. Citations of Saint-Marc Girardin, *Cours de littérature dramatique, ou de l'usage des passions dans le drame*, vol. 1 [1843] (Paris: Charpentier, 6th ed., 1857), 188–9, 205; Joseph de Maistre, *Les Soirées de Saint-Pétersbourg* (1821), 5th dialogue, in *Œuvres*, ed. Pierre Glaudes (Paris: Laffont, 2007), 588. De Maistre applied the expression 'human prelude to the Gospel' not to the pagan authors, but to Plato's philosophy.

of the tragedy was precisely what the eminent curator at the Cabinet des Médailles took exception to. No, Charles Lenormant exclaims, contrary to what the Moderns would have us believe, Oedipus is anything but a model of morality:

> He is an object of respect and even adoration for super-stition, not because he has made amends for involuntary crimes, imposed by Fate, through personal virtues and the exercise of his free will, but because he combines, in the series of crimes to which he is forced to admit, all the clauses with which the theology of pantheism had sought to express divine action on natural phenomena, the succession of beings, the reaction of the spirit on the matter that produced it, the imperfection of created things, the balance of the world, based on the discord of the elements that compose it, and the perpetual flux into which blind chance sweeps every exist-ence and reduces absolute existence to the identical nature of being and non-being, life and death.

'Superstition': the word has been spoken. Thus the tomb of Oedipus, 'the final asylum of a man whose story contains and personifies all of religion', is really the epitome of all the most vile beliefs of ancient paganism:

> This hidden grave, placed under the protection of the Eumenides, above which rises the altar to Titan, he who stole fire from the sky; before which Theseus and Pirithous, who typify friendship in the way that Oedipus's sons represent discord, placed the monument to their alliance before descending into Hades, where they will remain eternally chained; a grave over which are worshipped Minerva and Neptune, creators of plant and animal life, and around which the plains are fertile, the waters fecund, the trees heavy with fruit, the pastures covered in vigorous herds – this grave with its secrets initially entrusted to the king of the

land and then passed down from generation to generation, like a privilege of the supreme magistracy, what could it be other than the collective image of religious faith, obscure, contradictory, impure, cruel, as paganism was by nature, and surrounded by fears, rites, silences all the more powerful because it was itself more mysterious, less chaste, less human, and more absurd?[13]

Which explains why, despite appearances, no play could be less appropriate for a Catholic establishment than *Oedipus at Colonus*. This was the scandal denounced by Lenormant at the very heart of an article supposed to contribute to ecclesiastical propaganda.

Only someone with an in-depth knowledge of ancient Greece in its least-stereotypical cultural and historical reality, shorn of the charming visions of the European neoclassical imagination, could swap the panegyrics expected of him for such an eloquent indictment of Sophocles's tragedy. It fell to an archaeologist to highlight all the differences that open an abyss between us and pagan Antiquity, and to recoil from that Antiquity with a horror intensified by the fact that in searching through its ruins with his own hands, he had intimately come to know its secrets.

Lenormant was certainly not the only thinker of his time to emphasize the radical strangeness of the very Greeks whose educational humanism was so widely touted. As we have seen, Müller preceded him on this path, while only a few years earlier Leconte de Lisle had published his *Poèmes antiques*, in which the poet sought to contest classically inspired idyllicism by restoring archaizing scenes more faithful to history.[14]

---

13 Lenormant, 'Œdipe à Colone', 708–9.
14 Leconte de Lisle, preface to *Poèmes antiques* (Paris: Ducloux, 1852), xvi–xvii.

It is remarkable that scholars such as Müller and Lenormant tried their hand at a structural anthropology scarcely
different from that which would come into fashion one century later, beginning in the 1950s, to achieve a defamiliarization
that would make the Greeks into the Moderns' new barbar-
ians. Consider the German philologist's interpretation of the
importance of crossroads in Oedipus's life and, especially,
Lenormant's beautiful analysis of the symbolic and religious
characteristics of this tomb's location, combining being
and not being, sky and underworld, concord and discord,
mineral, plant, and animal: it is easily on a par with the structuralist exegesis by Pierre Vidal-Naquet in the 1970s.[15]

In his article about Sophocles's play, Charles Lenormant
also describes his visit a few years earlier to the site of Colonus
and the 'hillock (*kolônê*) that gave the village its name':

> At its summit is a modest chapel, before which rests the great
> German antiquarian, the author of the best history of Greek
> poetry, Karl Otfried Müller, killed by the Greek sun and
> overwork. Sitting before his grave, to my right I could see the
> Cephissus wandering off into a thousand channels through
> the dense gardens that have replaced the sacred wood of the
> Eumenides, and in front of me I glimpsed the ancient crenels
> of the Acropolis, crowned by the top of the Parthenon.[16]

The French archaeologist could not know that he would
have all of eternity to contemplate this landscape, being
destined to join in death the German colleague upon whose
grave he reflected. Müller died of sunstroke; Lenormant
caught a chill after a storm in Epidaurus and died in Athens

---

15   Pierre Vidal-Naquet, 'Oedipus Between Two Cities: An Essay on
Oedipus at Colonus', in Jean-Pierre Vernant and Pierre Vidal-Naquet,
Myth and Tragedy in Ancient Greece, trans. Janet Lloyd (New York: Zone
Books, 1988), 358. See above, Chapter 1, 'The Place', 3.
16   Lenormant, '*Œdipe à Colone*', 690.

on 24 November 1859, during a trip to introduce his son to the wonders of Greece.[17] The hero of Colonus claimed his dues: by a twist of fate, the tomb of Oedipus so passionately hated by the Christian scholar became his own grave – or at least the place where his heart was interred. The jealous hero thus called back to himself the man who had spurned him and uncovered his secrets: one cannot betray the mysteries of the gods with impunity.

The Gospel According to Sophocles

Yet for all his efforts, Lenormant alone could never have refuted the Christian interpretation of *Oedipus at Colonus*: we have just seen how popular it was with the French church. In Germany, the likes of Catholic philologist and philosopher Ernst von Lasaulx were effusively on board:

> The hero Oedipus reigning as a benefactor after his death is none other than Christian gnosis resuscitated above the tomb of Hellenic philosophy, which is its constant base; for all of pagan knowledge must disappear into death for the immortal Christian truth to be born.[18]

An opportune image of death and resurrection, one that allows a remarkable theological vagueness to persist regarding the

---

17   See Henri Wallon, 'Notice historique sur la vie et les travaux de M. Charles Lenormant, membre de l'Académie des inscriptions et belles-lettres', *Mémoires de l'Institut National de France: Académie des inscriptions et belles-lettres*, vol. 31 (Paris: Imprimerie nationale, 1884), 547–608.

18   Ernst von Lasaulx, 'Über den Sinn der Oedipussage', in *Verzeichnis der Vorlesungen, welche an der königlich-bayerischen Julius-Maximilians-Universität zu Würzburg im Sommersemester 1841 gehalten werden* (Würzburg: Thein, 1841), 13; reissued in *Studien des classichen Alterthums: Akademische Abhandlungen* (Regensburg: Manz, 1854), 373.

question of the exact relationship between paganism and Christianity as supposedly illustrated by the tomb of Oedipus. After all, the Hegelian dialectics that inspired Lasaulx also included carefully chosen grey areas that enabled the introduction of an ad hoc 'sublation' (*Aufhebung*) between two stages of an argument. Rome added this gnostic of the new school to the Index: among his misdeeds, turning Oedipus into a kind of pagan Christ ultimately seemed a step too far.

Yet the pontifical condemnation was futile: interpretations of *Oedipus at Colonus* in a Christian, even downright evangelical, light long continued to proliferate. As late as 1957, the Hellenist Georges Méautis, a professor at the University of Neuchâtel, brooked no restraint: according to him, if Sophocles turned Oedipus into a source of salvation and painted him as a 'beggar, wretched because he passed through the "dark night", because he has been rejected, reviled, considered an object of horror', it was because he sensed 'that beyond the Flagellation, beyond the crown of thorns, the Stations of the Cross, the Crucifixion, the distress of "Father, why have you forsaken me?" lies the mystery of resurrection'. To believe Méautis, Greek tragedy in general is nothing but 'the prefiguration of the drama of Calvary'.[19]

If that is true, then there is nothing for it but to slot the tragedian among the prophets of the Old Testament. Is Oedipus not a dead ringer for the Suffering Servant sung by Isaiah?[20]

---

19 Georges Méautis, *Sophocle: Essai sur le héros tragique* (Paris: Albin Michel, 1957), 171, 293.
20 Isaiah 53.

Tragedy and Ecstasy

To counter this persistent Christianizing tradition, many philologists strove to underscore everything that was fundamentally non-Christian, or even anti-Christian, about tragedy in general and *Oedipus at Colonus* in particular. The word was that if an effort was made to reframe tragedy in the context of ancient paganism, the Gospel according to Sophocles would not survive.

Müller and Lenormant opened the way; Paul Yorck von Wartenburg made a decisive advance. As a student at the University of Breslau in 1856, he had met Jacob Bernays, then a professor at the university. This was the period when the great philologist was preparing his paper on catharsis in Aristotle:[21] this coincidence would shape the doctoral thesis Yorck defended nine years later. In it Yorck set out to verify whether the Aristotelian theory of catharsis could concretely be applied to a tragedy. The example he chose was *Oedipus at Colonus*. Borrowing Bernays's physiological interpretation of catharsis, Yorck was inspired (possibly by Müller)[22] to connect it with the Cult of Dionysus, of which the tragic performances of Athens were an integral part.

According to the young scholar, catharsis was a mere consequence of the ecstasy that took hold of believers in Dionysus. As a communion with the forces of nature, this ecstasy aroused negative emotions – terror, pain, desire – of which the soul purified itself as they successively appeared.[23] Through ecstasy, through participation in 'the current of

21 See K. Gründer, *Zur Philosophie des Grafen Paul Yorck von Wartenburg: Aspekte und neue Quellen* (Göttingen: Vandenhoeck & Ruprecht, 1970), 99. On Bernays's work, see above, Chapter 3, 'The Body'.
22 Müller, 'Über den Inhalt', 191–2.
23 Paul Yorck von Wartenburg, *Die Katharsis des Aristoteles und der Oedipus Coloneus des Sophokles* (Berlin: Hertz, 1866), 22–4.

forces flooding the universe'[24] or in what Lenormant described above as 'the perpetual flux into which blind chance sweeps every existence', as well as through the identification with fate found in tragedy, the individual achieved a salutary forgetting of self. But this salutary effect only lasted a short while:

> The production of ecstasy: that is the vocation of ancient tragedy, which long met a need of pre-Christian humanity because it enabled humans through the ecstatic forgetting of self to experience a reduction, however brief, of the suffering tied to the god. – But in awakened man, a new torment awoke. History teaches us that the awareness of having been abandoned by the god, which was the final fate in the ancient world, threatened to lead to the annihilation of the humanity that was seized by [this realization]; – and it is then that the occurrence of Redemption took place.[25]

Like Lenormant, Yorck does not conceal his religious perspective: in his interpretative framework, directly inspired by the Christian history of salvation, Oedipus appears as an emblematic figure of paganism. He is 'the image of the human being', struggling against a fate personified by the Eumenides:

> The blind old man walks without support and without a guide, followed by those who see, until he reaches the wood of the goddesses of fate, and he disappears into the darkness of the sanctuary. Coming out of the night of fate, the human being is born in the light, the shadows of fate obscure his life, until he returns to the night from which he came.[26]

24 Ibid., 21–2.
25 Ibid., 37.
26 Ibid., 33.

For Yorck, Greek tragedy represents the highest theological expression of human consciousness before the advent of Christianity; a consciousness threatened by the feeling of divine dereliction.[27] Nevertheless, contrary to what has been said, Yorck does not read the tragic text as 'a kind of proto-Gospel':[28] that would be Lasaulx's thesis. On the contrary, Yorck emphasizes the fact that there is nothing Christian about this theatre:

> Here we encounter the limits of ancient consciousness, up against which comes our Christian way of seeing things, which is superior and which demands, to speak with Hegel, that the heart make itself the tomb of the heart.[29]

In other words, tragedy is pre-Christian, so long as we insist on that prefix.

Though this interpretation contained few absolutely original elements, it was the first to offer a synthesis of three previously distinct types of analyses of tragedy: the Hegelian philosophy of history, Müller's history of ancient myths and religion, and Bernays's philological standard. In fact, Yorck's account was not entirely satisfactory in its approach to any of these fields – and particularly not the third. Yet its historical importance proved considerable, for the simple reason that soon after its publication in 1866, it encountered a reader of genius: Nietzsche himself, who twice borrowed his fellow scholar's thesis from the university library at Basel: in May 1870, and again in February 1871, during the period when he was working on *The Birth of Tragedy* (published in 1872). The similarities between the two works are striking:

---

27 Ibid., 20–1.
28 Gründer, *Zur Philosophie des Grafen Paul Yorck von Wartenburg*, 103.
29 Yorck von Wartenburg, *Die Katharsis des Aristoteles*, 32–3. The reader will have recognized the Hegel text cited above.

both return Attic tragedy to the context of the Cult of Dionysus, describe tragic ecstasy as an obliteration of individual feeling, and define a strictly tragic age of human consciousness. The divergences between the two thinkers are ultimately less related to their general analysis than to the value systems they apply to it: while Yorck rejoices to see Christianity bring the tragic era to an end, Nietzsche is dispirited by the fact that Socrates laid it to rest.[30] Regarding a reality that remains identical, only the point of view changes.

The Battle of Verse 1583

After Hegel, Müller, and Lenormant, and after Lasaulx, Yorck von Wartenburg, and Nietzsche, we can no longer think about tragedy without considering its religious dimension. *Oedipus at Colonus* has a special place in this debate, which is no surprise, given that few tragedies offer such a continuous development of the theme of rites and the divine.

However, this controversial field has been riddled with so many interpretative abuses over the last two centuries that philologists have become extremely – even excessively – touchy: these matters are often surrounded by something close to a taboo, despite the fact that an accurate assessment of the texts' religious value is essential if we are properly to read and establish them.

A case in point would be the mysterious verses 1583 and 1584 of *Oedipus at Colonus*. An envoy comes to describe

---

30 Gründer, *Zur Philosophie des Grafen Paul Yorck von Wartenburg*, 105. See also Luca Crescenzi, 'Philologie und deutsche Klassik: Nietzsche als Leser von Paul Graf Yorck von Wartenburg', in *'Centauren-Geburten': Wissenschaft, Kunst und Philosophie beim jungen Nietzsche*, ed. Tilman Borsche, Federico Gerratana and Aldo Venturelli (Berlin: De Gruyter, 1994), 208–16. On Nietzsche and *The Birth of Tragedy*, see Marx, *L'Adieu à la littérature: Histoire d'une dévalorisation (XVIIIe–XXe siècle)* (Paris: Minuit, 2005), 83–9; *Vie du lettré* (Paris: Minuit, 2009), 129–37.

the circumstances of Oedipus's death to the inhabitants of Colonus. To the chorus's question, 'Did the unfortunate one die?', all the manuscripts have the messenger reply: 'Know that he has *left* (*leloipota*) the eternal life (*ton aei bioton*)', which does not make much sense, unless one assumes that Sophocles was attempting a surrealist drama. The passage already seemed problematic as early as Antiquity. While scholiasts suggested that *ton aei bioton* could be read as 'his long old age' (*to makron gêras*), this was really forcing the words. In short, the text seemed forever compromised.

And there things would have remained, if around 1760 a Plymouth clergyman by the name of Zachariah Mudge had not entrusted his notes on Sophocles to his friend Benjamin Heath, who was preparing an edition of commentary and lessons on the Greek tragedians, and if Heath had not included in his book Mudge's elegant and clever suggestion to substitute *lelogkhota* for *leloipota*.[31] Everything then becomes clear, for the messenger's reply now reads: 'Know that he has *obtained* (*lelogkhota*) eternal life.'

Everything becomes clear – or obscured. At the beginning of the nineteenth century, the great German scholar Gottfried Hermann, the leading figure of lexical and grammatical philology, sarcastically pummelled this hypothesis, qualifying 'Mudge's conjecture that rewards Oedipus with the eternal life of Christians' as 'inept'.[32] Here is indeed the problem: does reading *lelogkhota* instead of *leloipota* mean permanently opting for a Christianizing interpretation of *Oedipus at Colonus*, worthy of Méautis and the minor

---

31   Benjamin Heath, *Notae sive lectiones ad tragicorum Graecorum veterum, Aeschyli, Sophoclis, Euripidis, quae supersunt dramata deperditorumque reliquias* (Oxford: Clarendon, 1762), V; *Notae sive lectiones ad Sophoclem*, 66.

32   Gottfried Hermann, ed. of Sophocles, *Oedipus Coloneus* [1825] (Leipzig: Fleischer, 2nd ed., 1841), 257.

seminar of Orléans? Does it turn the blind old man into a sort of Jesus Christ *avant la lettre*?

Given what was at stake, the ensuing battle around these few words comes as no surprise. In 1825, Eduard Wunder cautiously wrote:

> It appears to me that Sophocles wanted to say nothing other than 'Oedipus left for the eternal life', though I do not deny that this is signified by these words in quite an unusual way.[33]

A few decades later, the editor who revised Wunder's work for a new edition censored this hypothesis, no doubt finding it too daring.[34] In 1863, August Meineke agreed with Hermann that Mudge had ultimately made the envoy's message 'worthier of a Christian than a pagan'.[35] In 1885, Richard Claverhouse Jebb threw in the towel: the passage seemed so hopeless to him that he preferred not to take sides.[36] The wise man's advice: when in doubt, abstain. Really?

What is startling is that the awkwardness around this passage remains perceptible to this day. In their 1992 Oxford edition, Hugh Lloyd-Jones and Nigel Guy Wilson return to the text of the manuscripts, justifying their decision by stating that *ton aei bioton* does not mean 'eternal life', as was mistakenly believed, but 'the life that Oedipus always led, namely that life that was at every moment full of trials'.[37]

---

33 Eduard Wunder, ed. of Sophocles, *Tragoediae septem* (Leipzig: Hartmann, 1825); cited by the Reverend C. E. Palmer, ed. of Sophocles, *The Œdipus Coloneus* (Cambridge: Deighton, Bell, 1860), 199.

34 See E. Wunder, ed. of Sophocles, *Tragoediae, Vol. I, S. III continens Oedipum Coloneum* (Leipzig: Teubner, 5th ed. revised by Nikolaus Wecklein, 1889), 137.

35 August Meineke, ed. of Sophocles, *Oedipus Coloneus* (Berlin: Weidmann, 1863), 201.

36 Jebb, *The Oedipus Coloneus*, 242–3.

37 H. Lloyd-Jones and Nigel Guy Wilson, ed. of Sophocles, *Fabulae* (Oxford: Clarendon, 1992), 423. This is also the lesson Lloyd-Jones

In this case, the *leloipota* of the manuscripts can indeed be kept – provided one accepts this rather forced reading.

A different version of the passage appeared across the Channel. In a 1960 edition in the Collection des Universités de France series, Alphonse Dain chose Mudge's conjecture (*lelogkhota*), and Paul Mazon translated: 'Know he has won a life that does not end.'[38] This 'life that does not end' is an extremely clever way to avoid the overly Christian connotations of 'eternal life'. But Mazon betrays the text, for a more accurate translation would read: 'He has won *the* life (or *this* life) that does not end.' The indefinite article probably seemed a less Christianizing – and less compromising – solution.

The 1996 Teubner edition, by Roger David Dawe, also goes for Mudge's option, but this audacity is tempered by the fact that the collection does not offer a translation: one therefore does not really know to which direction Dawe's reading of the two verses inclines.[39]

What a strange problem in establishing a text, where objectivity seems impossible and no one is able to achieve the necessary distance! The entire debate seems polluted by Hermann's vigorous intervention cited above: to substitute *lelogkhota* for *leloipota* would favour a Christian reading of the play. Rather than commit such an unforgivable anachronism, some prefer to force the meaning of the words, as Lloyd-Jones and Wilson do. Anything rather than be caught, aspergillum in hand, baptizing Oedipus and Sophocles like Virgil and Aeneas were baptized in the Middle Ages: in this regard, Mazon's scruples are plain.

---

follows in the Loeb Classical Library (Cambridge, MA: Harvard University Press, 1994).

38 Sophocle, *Œdipe à Colone*, ed. Alphonse Dain, trans. Paul Mazon [1960], revised by Jean Irigoin (Paris: Belles Lettres, 'Collection des universités de France', 1990), 143: 'Sache qu'il a conquis une vie qui ne finit pas.'

39 Roger David Dawe, ed. of Sophocles, *Oedipus Coloneus* (Stuttgart: Teubner, 1996), 80.

But has the question been properly posed? Does 'the eternal life' (*ton aei bioton*) mentioned by the messenger necessarily refer, as these brilliant philologists surmised, to the Christian hereafter? It is highly unlikely, and this may be where the limits of a philology that focuses on words, rather than opening itself to all the realities of ancient life, become apparent. For it is not true that all heroes die. In Greek mythology, many vanish from the face of the earth without ever dying: some, like Menelaus, are carried away to the Isles of the Blessed; others, like Ganymede, are directly moved to Olympus; yet others are swallowed by the earth and dwell underground.

The third group's fate presents striking similarities to that of Oedipus: Amphiaraus is swallowed by the earth with his chariot and horses when Zeus opens a chasm beneath his wheels and he becomes immortal below; after meeting a similar fate, Trophonius predicts the future for anyone who comes to question him in a cave; Caeneus splits the earth with a kick and falls straight down, still alive, into the depths; Althaemenes also disappears into an abyss. Nietzsche's friend Erwin Rohde lists many other examples.[40] Sophocles writes that in the underworld Amphiaraus 'reigns driven by all his strength of life' (*pampsukhos anassei*),[41] while Xenophon states that 'he is venerated throughout his eternal life' (*aei zôn timasthai*).[42] This eternal life is

---

40 Erwin Rohde, *Psyche: The Cult of Souls and Belief in Immortality among the Greeks* (*Psyche: Seelencult und Unsterblichkeitsglaube der Griechen*, 1890–94), trans. W. B. Hillis (London: Kegan Paul, Trench, Trubner & Co., 1925), 89–92. See also Angelo Brelich, *Gli eroi greci: Un problema storico-religioso* (Rome: Edizioni dell'Ateneo, 1958), 87–8.

41 Sophocles, *Electra*, v. 841. *Pampsukhos* can be given different readings, but the movement of the dialogue and the argumentation rule out the kind of restrictive meaning given by Mazon in his translation for the Collection des Universités de France [1958] (Paris: Belles Lettres, 1989), 168: 'he reigns, but he is no more than a soul'.

42 Xenophon, *On Hunting*, I, 8. Following on from Dindorf, the *aei zôn* in the manuscripts has sometimes been corrected as *aeizôs*: this is a

surprisingly similar to the one Oedipus is granted at Colonus and, most importantly, owes nothing to Christianity.

My aim here is not to throw my support behind either option regarding verses 1583 and 1584: there is even less reason to choose between *leloipota* and *lelogkhota*, given that other conjectures have been proposed which make it possible to maintain the *leloipota* found in the manuscripts while getting rid of this supposedly troublesome 'eternal life'.[43] A discussion of this technically complex issue would be far beyond the scope of this volume.

The point to remember is only this: the terms of this debate were distorted from the start, the entire discussion having very quickly shifted to the question of determining whether or not a Christian interpretation of the play was legitimate. If it were true, as Hermann stated, that *ton aei bioton* inevitably had to refer to the 'eternal life' of Christianity, then one could understand the reticence displayed by editors and translators. But this is hardly the case: with all due respect to many philologists, immortality is in no way the exclusive privilege of Christianity, particularly since many pagan gods were said to enjoy it. In other words, the argument that Mudge's conjecture Christianizes the text lacks merit and, most importantly, offers insufficient grounds to dismiss this lesson.

Having failed to understand the real religious foundation of *Oedipus at Colonus* and perhaps even of tragedy in general, editors were unable to follow reason and objectively choose the most likely lesson. If we truly want to understand

---

way of tempering the expression's Christian connotation (see Edgar Cardew Marchant, ed. [1920] of Xénophon, *Opera omnia*, vol. 5 [Oxford: Clarendon, 1992], 180). In the Collection des Universités de France, Édouard Delebecque opts for an even more radical solution, and completely changes the expression (Paris: Belles Lettres, 1970), 52: how far will this fear of Christianizing pagan texts go?

43 See Hermann, ed., *Oedipus Coloneus*, and Meineke, ed., *Oedipus Coloneus*, notably 119 and 201.

tragedy, it is high time we overcame the simplistic binary that opposes paganism and Christianity and took a dispassionate look at Oedipus's fate, taking into account everything we know today about Greek religion at the time of Sophocles. We must recognize that neither Zachariah Mudge nor Gottfried Hermann has the answer.

Ritualists and Anti-Ritualists, at Cambridge and Elsewhere

It is no wonder that certain specialists seek to skirt the question of the religious basis of tragedy, in view of some of the grotesque positions it has generated over the last century.

On the one side, we have the 'Cambridge Ritualists'. Influenced by the work of James Frazer and Émile Durkheim, led by the Hellenists Jane Ellen Harrison and Gilbert Murray (who did not teach at Cambridge with Harrison, but at Oxford),[44] they related most of the social and cultural realities of ancient Greece to rites that had supposedly left their mark on them. Or, more precisely – for this is an unmistakeable case of reductionism – to a single rite: that of the 'Year Spirit' (*eniautos daimon*) who resembles Osiris, Attis, or Dionysus himself, in that he lives, dies, and is periodically reborn according to the agricultural cycle.[45]

In an appendix he added to Harrison's masterwork, *Themis*, published in 1912, Murray claimed to identify a structure common to the action of every tragedy. After a conflict (*agôn*) pitting the divinity against its enemies, the divinity experiences

---

44 See Robert Ackerman, 'The Cambridge Group: Origins and Composition', in *The Cambridge Ritualists Reconsidered*, ed. William M. Calder III, in *Illinois Classical Studies*, Supplement 2 (Atlanta: Scholars Press, 1991), 1–19.

45 See Jane Ellen Harrison, *Themis: A Study of the Social Origins of Greek Religion* (Cambridge: Cambridge University Press, 1912), 331–2.

the Passion (*pathos*) in the form of a sacrificial death; a messenger (*aggelos*) comes to announce the death, which leads to funerary lamentations (*thrênos*); finally there is an unexpected reversal of a situation or incident (*peripeteia*), which leads to the resurrection, apotheosis, or epiphany of the divinity: what Murray calls theophany.[46] This clever attempt to synthesize every tragedy into a single outline is all the more admirable given how few tragedies actually comply with it to the letter. *Oedipus at Colonus* fits the framework without too much difficulty, if one overlooks the fact that Oedipus's death is not a consequence of the conflicts that preceded it and that the theophany remains veiled in ambiguity.

Murray's theory was tremendously influential, particularly in English-speaking countries. Predictably enough it aroused equally strong opposition, from Arthur Pickard-Cambridge, who in 1927 launched a systematic takedown of the ritualist doctrine,[47] to Ivan Mortimer Linforth, who in 1951 sought to establish that a play like *Oedipus at Colonus* was absolutely not a religious drama.

Though they were widely noticed upon publication, these counterattacks did not have the long-term success one might have expected. In 1962, ten years after Pickard-Cambridge's death, his book was reissued in an edition by a colleague who cut nearly all the objections to Murray's arguments: *sic transit gloria mundi.*[48]

---

46 Gilbert Murray, 'Excursus on the Ritual Forms Preserved in Greek Tragedy', in ibid., 342–3.

47 Arthur Wallace Pickard-Cambridge, *Dithyramb, Tragedy and Comedy* (Oxford: Clarendon Press, 1927), 329–52. On criticism of Murray, see R. Ackerman, *The Myth and Ritual School: J. G. Frazer and the Cambridge Ritualists* (New York: Garland, 1991), 59–181; Rainer Friedrich, 'Everything to Do with Dionysos? Ritualism, the Dionysiac, and the Tragic', in *Tragedy and the Tragic: Greek Theatre and Beyond*, ed. M. S. Silk (Oxford: Clarendon Press, 1996), 260–1.

48 A. W. Pickard-Cambridge, *Dithyramb, Tragedy and Comedy*, 2nd ed., revised by Thomas Bertram Lonsdale Webster (Oxford: Clarendon Press, 1962), 126–9.

THE GOD

As for Linforth, while he was probably right to oppose those who saw Oedipus as the nearly Judeo-Christian personification of a 'suffering humanity' sanctified by its pain,[49] his objections went much too far, due to his rigid conception of ancient drama and systematic rejection of all the play's religious allusions as irrelevant.

'If the fortunes of Oedipus were recognized as determined by an inevitable fate *and nothing more*,' he wrote, 'the drama called *Oedipus at Colonus* would not exist.'[50] Clearly, Linforth was relying on an overly restrictive idea of what a Greek tragedy should be – an idea, moreover, highly influenced by the form of the modern drama, which attributes a decisive importance to the hero's freedom. For instance, Linforth decrees that the Eumenides are not essential in the play: this a pure argument from authority, stated against all evidence. He believes he has identified an essentially psychological framework to the tragedy, but this is more than debatable.[51] His conclusion:

Theologically, Sophocles does not discern or disclose any compensation for Oedipus; dramatically, he produces the illusion of it.[52]

A perfectly nonsensical conclusion, given that Sophocles is a dramatist, not an author of theological treatises: the only theology he can produce is of a dramatic order. One cannot

49 Werner Jaeger, *Paideia: La formation de l'homme grec* (*Paideia*, vol. 1, 1934), French trans. André and Simonne Devyver (1964) (Paris: Gallimard, 1988), 331. See also Lewis Campbell, *Religion in Greek Literature: A Sketch in Outline* (London: Longmans, 1898), 281. Cited by Ivan Mortimer Linforth, *Religion and Drama in 'Oedipus at Colonus'*, University of California Publications in Classical Philology, vol. 14, no. 4, (Berkeley: University of California Press, 1951), 78.
50 Linforth, 'Religion and Drama', 91.
51 Ibid., 94–7, 108–9, 114, and passim.
52 Ibid., 184.

distinguish between these two planes the way the American critic does: if the drama produces an illusion of compensation, then that compensation does have a theological significance, for the theatre is never anything but illusion and can only produce illusions. But these are significant illusions.

A list of all the preconceptions and illogical arguments in Linforth's reasoning makes it hard to understand how such a fragile stance exerted such a strong influence on readers of Sophocles, unless it was simply down to the peremptory harangues with which the Hellenist hammered it home, using the full weight of his seventy-two years. Or unless his article served to crystallize the scruples of an entire generation of philologists who were over the excesses of the ritualist theories and Christianizing interpretations of tragedy: we have seen how reticent suddenly ultra-sensitive scholarly temperaments could become when it came to religious matters.

But it is too easy to swing from one extreme to the other. Luckily, the current of ideas also changes direction from time to time and scholars today readily acknowledge the abuses of the anti-ritualist and anti-religious reaction promoted by Pickard-Cambridge, Linforth, and their ilk.[53]

Not that the debate has really ended. On the contrary, one still finds echoes of it in the current discussion pitting Pierre Judet de La Combe, advocate of a philosophical reading of tragedy, against Florence Dupont, who favours placing tragedy back in its ritual context.[54] The most fiercely ritualist theories, for their part, have found refuge in the theatre world, where practitioners influenced by Jane Harrison and

---

53 See Charles Segal, *Sophocles' Tragic World: Divinity, Nature, Society* (Cambridge, MA: Harvard University Press, 1995), 54; Friedrich, 'Everything to Do with Dionysos?'

54 Florence Dupont, *L'Insignifiance tragique* (Paris: Le Promeneur, 2001), 16–27; Pierre Judet de La Combe, *Les tragédies grecques sont-elles tragiques? Théâtre et théorie* (Paris: Bayard, 2010).

Gilbert Murray (but also by Antonin Artaud) have since the 1960s and '70s striven tirelessly to re-immerse their art in the sources of ritual and ceremony – mythical or otherwise, it scarcely matters, so long as they are effective. For if rituals can disappear, why cannot they be reborn? Even wrong-headed readings of tragedy can be useful and productive: tragic theatre's entire posterity is made of just such miracles.

'Nothing to Do with Dionysus'

All this wrangling only makes it more difficult to examine calmly the relationship between tragedy and religion. Here, we must tread cautiously: hypotheses and avenues for reflection are preferable to inflexible and definitive proposals.

The first question to settle (or to leave open) concerns Dionysus: what is the relationship between this god and tragedy? The question is poorly put, because it covers two different problems. The first pertains to the role of tragedy in the Dionysian ritual. Regarding this, objective data is plentiful and an answer easily arrived at: in fifth-century-BCE Athens, tragic performances were an integral part of the ceremonies in honour of the god, in particular during the winter Lenaia, but most importantly in spring, during the City Dionysia. After a procession (*pompê*) and a sort of carnival (*kômos*), a three-day competition was held during which three poets each presented a tetralogy composed of three tragedies followed by a drama whose characters were satyrs. During these three days, a competition of comedies was also held, which extended into the next two days and was accompanied among other things by a competition of hymns to Dionysus: the dithyrambs.[55] There can be absolutely no

---

55 This is a very basic description of the organization of the City Dionysia in Athens in the fifth century BCE. For more details, notably on

doubt that the tragic competition was an essential component of the festivities held in honour of the god.

But we must be clear about the meaning of this reality. Are we dealing with a simple external coincidence between two events, or a deeper coherence? In other words, was tragedy as consubstantially linked with the Dionysian celebrations as the performances of the Passion at Oberammergau are with the Christian liturgy? Or was the relationship between the two as tenuous as that between the resurrection of Christ and the contemporary Foire du Trône in Paris? Merry-go-round operators and waffle vendors at the Foire du Trône would be surprised to learn that their event was founded to celebrate Easter. The truth of an event is not necessarily found in its origin: even if we knew the circumstances under which tragedy was invented, its meaning would not be elucidated and the way in which it was experienced would remain a mystery.

This brings us to the second aspect of the question asked above. If theatre played an important role in the Dionysian ritual, what about the reverse? In other words, what was the place of ritual and of Dionysus himself in tragedy? The answer to this question would also reveal the reason these tragic competitions existed.

All sorts of hypotheses have sprung up. Yorck and Nietzsche saw the god as the deity of tragic ecstasy and intoxication par excellence; Jean-Pierre Vernant described him as the god of tragic fiction;[56] Harrison and Murray recognized

the other theatrical festivals held in honour of Dionysus, see A. W. Pickard-Cambridge, *The Dramatic Festivals of Athens* [1953] (Oxford: Clarendon Press, 2nd ed. revised, 1988); Natale Spineto, *Dionysos a teatro: Il contesto festivo del dramma greco* (Rome: L'Erma di Bretschneider, 2004).

56 Jean-Pierre Vernant, 'The God of Tragic Fiction' [1981], in Jean-Pierre Vernant and Pierre Vidal-Naquet, *Myth and Tragedy in Ancient Greece*, trans. Janet Lloyd (New York: Zone Books, 1988). See also Friedrich, 'Everything to Do with Dionysos?', 257–83, and, in the same volume, Richard Seaford's response, 'Something to Do with Dionysos – Tragedy and

Dionysus as an incarnation of their famous 'Year Spirit' tied to the agrarian cycle. In fact, there are as many opinions as there are philologists. The triumph of free interpretation.

The Ancients were wiser than the Moderns in maintaining a fitting reserve on this point: according to them, tragedy was 'nothing to do with Dionysus'.[57] The phrase was said to go back to the distant era when the poets Phrynichus and Aeschylus were the first to devote their writings to a wide variety of mythological figures, heroes and divinities, rather than to the god of wine and inebriation usually celebrated. It had since become a saying, applied to anyone talking about what they did not know.

The fact is that among the tragedies that have survived, only one features Dionysus as a character, and that is Euripides's *The Bacchae*, which was not first staged in Athens.[58] Even among the lost plays whose titles are known to us, rare are the subjects related to the god. At the end of the fifth century, Athenians had come to terms with the idea that tragedy was not about Dionysus and that its relationship with the great Dionysian ceremonies was purely fortuitous.

Yet this does not mean that we must adopt this radical point of view today; one is always free to try to uncover or invent a coherence that was not evident to tragedy's spectators in Antiquity. Without picking and choosing among what are ultimately rather fragile hypotheses, there is a

the Dionysiac: Response to Friedrich', in Silk, *Tragedy and the Tragic*, 284–94; Pat E. Easterling, 'A Show for Dionysus', in *The Cambridge Companion to Greek Tragedy*, ed. P. E. Easterling (Cambridge: Cambridge University Press, 1997), 36–53.

57 Zenobius, *Proverbs*, v. 40, in *Corpus paroemiographorum Graecorum*, ed. Ernst Ludwig von Leutsch and Friedrich Wilhelm Schneidewin (Göttingen: Vandenhoeck, 1839), 137: 'Ouden pros ton Dionuson.' Plutarch provides an interrogative version of the adage, *Table-Talk*, I, 1, 5, 615 a: 'What has this to do with Dionysus?' (Ti tauta pros ton Dionuson?)

58 See Henri Grégoire, 'Notice' [1961], in Euripide, *Les Bacchantes* (Paris: Belles Lettres, 1993), 11–14.

simple observation to be made, which echoes the principal argument made by Nietzsche and Vernant: as the god of mystical ecstasy and transcendence of self, Dionysus was more liable to preside over theatrical performances than any other god of ancient Greece, with the possible exception of Hermes, god of deception and lies.

To which a second observation may be added: Dionysus was the only god who had to go to some lengths to establish his own cult, and he only succeeded after overcoming numerous obstacles. All the other great divinities, apart from Zeus, had been recognized as such from the moment of their birth – which was admittedly not always without peril – and had fully exercised their divine rights from the beginning. Unlike his fellow deities, Dionysus had a *story*. His life had ups and downs. It followed a direction: one could use a map to track his progress across the world as he spread his cult. Like Heracles, he had had to undergo numerous trials. Of all the gods, his was the closest to a hero's life: it is said that the women of Elis sang, 'Come, *hero* Dionysus.'[59]

It follows that were a god eventually to become the god of theatrical ecstasy as well as of tragic adventure and incident, none would have been better suited than Dionysus. This is the outcome reached by eliminating the other divinities: a meagre haul. More tangible certainties are beyond our reach: all the rest consist of hypotheses, each more tempting than the last, but a hypothesis nonetheless.

---

59 Plutarch, *The Greek Questions*, 36: 'elthein, hêrô Dionuse'. The emphasis is mine, of course. This is the text of the manuscripts, which is contested by contemporary editors, on the grounds that Dionysus is not a hero (Jacques Boulogne [Paris: Belles Lettres, 2002], 415). But this precise point deserves to be qualified: see Karl Kerényi, 'Prolegomena zu einer Darstellung der Heroenmythologie der Griechen', *Saeculum* 7 (1956): 391–4; Brelich, *Gli eroi greci*, 368.

A Heroic Trial by Ordeal

But what if we were approaching the problem backwards? Since Dionysus's only deep connection to tragedy is through his heroic nature, in that he is the most human of all the gods, why not see this as the raison d'être for a tragic performance less specifically tied to the Dionysian ritual than to the cult of heroes in general?

This was the theory initially put forward by the archaeologist William Ridgeway in a 1904 conference, then picked up by Gilbert Murray before he and Jane Harrison lost themselves in the mysteries of the 'Year Spirit': one of the possible origins of tragedy, Murray wrote, could have been 'the ritual performed in so many parts of Greece at the grave of an ancestor or dead hero'.[60] For instance, Herodotus reports that in Sicyon, in the Peloponnesus, it was customary for 'tragic choruses' to commemorate the misfortunes (*pathea*) of the hero who founded the city, Adrastus, in place of Dionysus.[61]

'Almost every tragedy, as a matter of fact', Murray continues, 'can be resolved into a lament over the grave of some canonized hero or heroine, mixed with a re-enacting of his death.' This explains the 'funereal tone' of tragedies and the 'ever-present shadow of death' that hovers over them and is apparently so little compatible with the scenes of Dionysian jubilation; most importantly, it reveals why 'there is an actual tomb present as a central fact of the story in the majority of tragedies'.[62] As Nicole Loraux has pointed out,

---

60 Gilbert Murray, 'Preface to the Third Edition' [1907], in *A History of Ancient Greek Literature* [1897] (London: Heinemann, 1917), xxv. See William Ridgeway, *The Origin of Tragedy, with Special Reference to the Greek Tragedians* (Cambridge: Cambridge University Press, 1910), 1–55.

61 Herodotus, *Histories*, V, 67, 26–30.

62 Murray, 'Preface to the Third Edition', xxv.

tragedy is profoundly connected with mourning, and it is a hero who is being mourned.[63]

But what in fact is a hero? A mortal to whom death has allowed access to a higher and supernatural rank, a deceased person who is the object of a cult. Unlike a god, the hero has a human body. Since the hero's body is not distinct from that of a man, he can be represented by one.

From here, we can allow ourselves to imagine the invention of tragedy. A chorus lamenting over a dead man. A sacrifice takes place, which allows contact with the deceased. Suddenly, a participant lets himself be inhabited by the spirit of the hero and manifests this possession in his body and even in his words; the mask helps this to happen, for it has the power to enable incarnation, to permit one to leave both oneself and the world – and Dionysus is the god of masks par excellence.[64] Finally, a dialogue is engaged with the chorus: tragedy is born. It is an origin myth as good as any other.

This process of incarnation will not surprise spectators of Noh drama: anyone who has seen the masked actor (*shite*) mysteriously emerge from the wings, and slowly glide onto the bridge leading to the stage, knows how a god walks. Why wouldn't tragedy have wielded a like power of invocation?

One thing is certain, in any case: in archaic Greece, the funeral rites of heroes and the powerful included funeral games in the form of competitions, which were often

---

63   Nicole Loraux, *La Voix endeuillée: Essai sur la tragédie grecque* (Paris: Gallimard, 1999).

64   See Jean-Pierre Vernant and Françoise Frontisi-Ducroux, 'Features of the Mask in Ancient Greece' [1983], in Vernant and Vidal-Naquet, *Myth and Tragedy in Ancient Greece*, 201–5; Françoise Frontisi-Ducroux, *Le Dieu-masque: Une figure du Dionysos d'Athènes* (Paris: La Découverte, 1991). See this account by a contemporary Noh actor: 'Before I begin to act . . . I have to look for many hours at the mask. I do not exist, the mask does. I am not real – the mask is real.' Quoted by Jan Kott, 'Noh, or about Signs', trans. Joanna Clark, *Arion* 1 (1973–74): 685.

THE GOD

athletic.[65] The Olympic Games, organized around relics of the hero Pelops, originated in this tradition which boasts its most illustrious literary example in the description of the funeral of Patroclus in Book XXIII of *The Iliad*. But these occasions also featured poetry competitions: Hesiod proudly recounts how he wrote a hymn that won the prize at a funeral competition in honour of the 'valiant Amphidamas'.[66]

As it happens, tragic performances at Athens's City Dionysia were also organized as competitions. Lots were drawn to select ten judges at random to represent the city's ten tribes. At the end of the three tetralogies, each judge ranked the plays on a tablet; the ten tablets were then placed in an urn; five were picked at random, and these five tablets dictated the final verdict.[67]

The awarding of prizes did not break with the prevailing system of democratic representation: as with the competitions, juries for trials were chosen at random. In this regard, Vernant and Vidal-Naquet are right to emphasize the political dimension of Athenian tragedy: it fully replicated the political operation of the city-state. But the random draw to select the five final tablets has too often been overlooked: it is the god who intervenes here. The god is the deciding arbiter of the competition. The tragic competition thus displays all the features of an ordeal, with the prize going to the tetralogy approved by the divinity.

The competition was a marvellous device: in a society rationally aiming for the ritual to be effective, it guaranteed that one offering would always be accepted. After all, people could never be sure that a sacrifice would be pleasing:

65 See Karl Meuli, 'Der Ursprung der Olympischen Spiele', *Die Antike* 17 (1941): 189–208, reissued in *Gesammelte Schriften*, ed. Thomas Gelzer (Basel: Schwabe, 1975), vol. 2, 881–905; Brelich, *Gli eroi greci*, 94–106; Pierre Lévêque, 'Approche ethno-historique des concours grecs', *Klio* 64, no. 1 (1982): 5–20.

66 Hesiod, *Works and Days*, v. 654–659.

67 See Pickard-Cambridge, *Dramatic Festivals of Athens*, 97.

impurity always threatened and the gods were so demanding, their preferences so arbitrary. With three offerings, however, it was a certainty that one of them would, at the minimum, be the least displeasing and not be rejected, even if it were not completely right. A guarantee was provided that divine favour would not be lost, for it would necessarily go to the least unworthy, if not the worthiest.

This was the mechanism of the tragic competition: it ensured that the deceased hero would have at least one successful incarnation and that the sacrifice would please him.

Tragedy as Tomb

In this funerary context, it comes as no surprise that the chthonic gods, or gods of the earth and its bowels, are so present in *Oedipus at Colonus* – Erinyes, Poseidon, and Hades. Even Zeus and Apollo appear primarily in their infernal form, as the telluric Zeus (*khthonios*) who makes the earth shake, and the Apollo of Delphi who inspires the Pythia from the depths of a mephitic crevice.

The play is basically a long preparation for the hero's death, or rather, according to Ridgeway's and Murray's explanatory blueprint, a ritual evocation of his final moments. Yet this is quite a curious funeral rite, organized around not a tomb but the absence of a tomb. If no libation can be poured, no funeral wreath laid, no chrysanthemum left on it, this tomb truly is, as Mallarmé would have put it, 'the one absent from every bouquet'.[68]

<hr/>

68 Stéphane Mallarmé, 'Crise de vers', in *Œuvres complètes*, ed. Bertrand Marchal (Paris: Gallimard, 'Bibliothèque de la Pléiade', 1998–2003), vol. 2, 213. English translation by Mary Ann Caws, ed., 'Crisis in Poetry', in *Mallarmé: Selected Poetry and Prose* (New York: New Directions, 1982), 76.

In this case, tragedy appears as the site of an impossible ritual. The title of Sophocles's last play means not only that Oedipus died at Colonus, but that he is still there, to this day, to the moment of the performance: with so many realistic geographic details allowing Athenians to locate the place of this disappearance, the drama functions as a record. But not only as that. The play also makes visible the hero's invisible tomb and preserves its memory: the tragedy itself constitutes Oedipus's real tomb, a tribute and memorial to an imperceptible but still effective supernatural presence. It makes possible – to quote Mallarmé again – an 'insubstantial grief'.[69]

It is a propitiatory play, like certain Noh dramas charged with attracting the favours of a god. In other words, and with all due respect to Linforth, there is little psychological drama here. When the tragedy begins, Oedipus has already made his choice: he will stay in Athens, at whatever cost; he knows the city will welcome him. From the beginning, the hero is in divine eternity, in the safety of those who entrust themselves to the gods, while Athens, represented by Theseus and the people of Colonus, is in the more human time of decision. From this perspective, the capital of Attica is the central human character while Oedipus already belongs to the world beyond.

Ultimately, the play only describes an exchange: in return for physical protection, Oedipus will offer a divine and supernatural protection. Since the counter-gift is far superior to the gift, Athens will derive by far the greater benefit from this barter or potlatch: it will become the holy city, and Theseus will be invested with Oedipus's aura.[70] If the

---

69 Stéphane Mallarmé, 'Tombeau', Œuvres complètes, vol. 1, 39. English: 'Tomb of Paul Verlaine', trans. Hubert Creekmore, Mallarmé, 53.

70 This shift of Oedipus's aura to Theseus is announced from a dramatic point of view by the fact that at the very end of the tragedy, given the constraints of distributing the parts among the three actors, the

tragedy truly alludes to a recent episode in the Peloponnesian War, when the Athenians had victoriously repelled a Theban attack near Colonus,[71] then it really works like an ex-voto offered to the protecting hero: it is a giving of thanks.

The last of the surviving tragedies returns to the original mission of the tragic choruses: the evocation of the illustrious dead. Sophocles may have consciously gone back to the sources of Attic drama. He could not have known that, twenty-four centuries later, *Oedipus at Colonus* would be the last tragedy to be rescued from the disappearance of Greek literature, but he might have been aware that it would be the last of his own works, given that he was then close to ninety years old. It is certainly relevant that Sophocles wrote a prose treatise on the chorus, now lost, in which it is said that he opposed Thespis and Choerilus, two of the inventors of tragic theatre.[72] We do not know what his thesis was. But it is not unlikely that Sophocles, who was unanimously reported to stand out for his extreme religiosity, reproached his two predecessors for de-ritualizing the chorus and launching a movement whereby theatre grew increasingly distant from its cultural origins. In his final masterpiece Sophocles wanted to show his contemporaries a new path, by which the reconciliation of drama and ritual would finally be possible, the evocation of the dead would return to the centre of the performance, and the cult of the hero would be relevant once more.

This is pure hypothesis, no doubt, and possibly even hypothesis based on hypotheses. The ground crumbles

---

character of Theseus inevitably had to be played by the actor who had played Oedipus throughout the play (the protagonist). This is also the point where Theseus takes on the role of substitute father to Antigone and Ismene.

71   Sophocles, *Oedipus at Colonus*, v. 1533–1534. See above, Chapter 1, 'The Place'.

72   See the 'Suda' entry on Sophocles, reproduced by Jacques Jouanna, *Sophocle* (Paris: Fayard, 2007), 688.

beneath our feet in a fine dust and flies up around us in thick volutes: this is as far as we can go in understanding Sophocles and his last play, *Oedipus at Colonus*.

From the 'Song of the He-Goat' to the *Agnus Dei*

Everything that follows is glimpsed through a dense fog, as if in a dream. Do not value it any more highly. Dreams mean something, but what?

For there does remain a mystery. Oedipus flouts every kind of law – familial (he kills his father and marries his mother), civic (he openly rejects Creon, the sovereign of Thebes), religious (he curses a supplicant, his own son Polynices) – and yet he remains a protégé of the gods. An apparently extraordinary situation: the weakest being, the one most stained with dishonour, turns into the most powerful and spreads his gifts left and right.

This happens to be the same metamorphosis as is undergone by the dreadful Erinyes to become the Eumenides, that is, 'the kindly ones'. It is no coincidence that the play is presented with an invocation to the Eumenides, for they illustrate the way the sacred can turn into its opposite through a kind of passage to the limit. Both Greek and Latin employ the same word for the holy and the cursed (*hagios*, *sacer*), as if these were two inseparable facets of a single reality. The Theban hero is the figure of transgression, of the passage from one state to the other.

The anthropologist René Girard sees this reversibility as the core principle of the myth of Oedipus:

> The mysterious union of the most evil and most beneficial forces is of vital concern to the community, and can be neither challenged nor ignored. Nevertheless, it is a paradox that totally escapes human comprehension; and religion

humbly acknowledges its impotence. The beneficial Oedipus at Colonus supersedes the earlier, evil Oedipus, but he does not negate him. How could he negate him, since it was the expulsion of a *guilty* Oedipus that prompted the departure of violence? The peaceful outcome of his expulsion confirms the justice of the sentence passed on him, his unanimous conviction for patricide and incest. If Oedipus is indeed the saver of the community, it is because he is a patricidal and incestuous son.[73]

The evil being turns into a source of salvation through an apotropaic mechanism well attested to elsewhere. In the Bible, for example, the bronze serpent lifted on the end of a stick suddenly becomes a beneficial figure that can prevent all snakebites – probably for the specific reason that a snake tied to a stick can no longer do any harm.[74] Sophocles therefore stages the system of the scapegoat or *pharmakos* with an acute consciousness of the workings of religious practice: in the same way that the word *pharmakon* refers to both the medicine and the poison, the *pharmakos* Oedipus (who gives, or acts as, the *pharmakon*) sometimes poisons and sometimes cures. He is the sorcerer or villain, but also the one who serves as a remedy by purifying others' ills and offering himself in sacrifice as a scapegoat.

This mechanism may explain the mystery of the site of Oedipus's tomb. No one but Theseus and his successors can know its exact location. As it happens, the object used to purify (*katharma*) had to be thrown over the user's shoulder while he looked away.[75] The concealment of the hero's death thus appears as the price to pay to make the *pharmakon*

---

73 René Girard, *La Violence et le sacré* [1972] (Paris: Hachette, 2002), 132. *Violence and the Sacred*, trans. Patrick Gregory (Baltimore: Johns Hopkins University Press, 1979), 86.

74 Numbers XXI, 4–9; John III, 14–15.

75 See Aeschylus, *The Libation Bearers*, v. 99–100.

effective. A painful price for Antigone and Ismene, unable to perform for their father the rites required, but a necessary one for the Athenians to enjoy its protective power.

As seductive as it might be, Girard's interpretation of *Oedipus at Colonus* is not without its flaws, for it is not compatible with the information delivered in the play. When an oracle of Apollo announces that the hero has become a source of salvation, the transformation is not attributed to an autonomous process: it is the gods who take pity on Oedipus for his suffering, the gods who 'raise him up now, when yesterday they struck him down'.[76] The character's final transfiguration is related to an external grace, the reversal of his circumstances to the intervention of divine mercy. There is nothing here like an internal mechanism whose workings remain secret, unless one supposes that out of ignorance the characters attribute to the benevolent action of the gods what in fact follows the principle of the victim as scapegoat. Girard's theory entails a hermeneutic duplicity in the play, with contradictory dual arguments, one of which is evident and the other esoteric.

The fact is that Girard offers less a reading than a deciphering or a decoding: he wants to reveal the hidden meaning of things – and in particular of tragedy. Given that the word *tragôidia* refers etymologically to a 'song of (or for) the he-goat' (*tragos*), an animal consecrated to Dionysus and immolated in his name, the temptation is strong to discern the memory of a rite of purification here, a purification through the intervention of a scapegoat. As Girard puts it: 'Greek tragedy, like the festival and indeed all other rites, is primarily a representation of sacrificial crisis and generative violence.'[77]

---

76 Sophocles, *Oedipus at Colonus*, v. 394. See also v. 383–384.
77 Girard, *La Violence et le sacré*, 132; *Violence and the Sacred*, 168.

The Libation Bearers, *Oedipus Rex*, and *Antigone* amply illustrate this theory. Although Clytemnestra and the two eponymous troublemaking heroes experience the punishment of death or exclusion, intended to re-establish public order, Clytemnestra is not really the cause of violence (that would be Agamemnon, who did not hesitate to sacrifice his daughter Iphigenia), and neither are Oedipus or Antigone: strictly speaking, they are no more than the designated hosts of a sacrifice intended to calm unrest. In other words, scapegoats.

Like all theories that claim to find the meaning of reality in a mythical origin, this theory has elicited and continues to elicit many criticisms.[78] Not the least of which is a reminder of our complete ignorance of whether or not he-goats were present during Dionysian ceremonies: the exact etymology of the word *tragedy* still remains a mystery.[79] The very existence of a sacrificial altar in the theatre is highly contested.

Another objection: precious few Athenian tragedies featured Athenian heroes. The myths that were staged mostly focused on enemy cities, primarily Thebes and Argos, whose misfortunes powerfully comforted the Attic capital – as if the Athenian audience left the theatre fortified by seeing the ordeals of its adversaries.[80] This is the case with the oldest surviving tragedy, *The Persians*, which recounts the defeat of King Xerxes by the Greeks. It is also true of the youngest,

---

78 See Richard Gordon, 'Reason and Ritual in Greek Tragedy: On René Girard, *Violence and the Sacred* and Marcel Detienne, *The Gardens of Adonis*', in *Comparative Criticism*, vol. 1, ed. Elinor Shaffer (Cambridge: Cambridge University Press, 1979): 279–310.

79 See Vernant, 'The God of Tragic Fiction', 184–5.

80 See Loraux, *La Voix endeuillée*, 67–82; Simon Goldhill, 'The Great Dionysia and Civic Ideology', and Froma I. Zeitlin, 'Thebes: Theater of Self and Society in Athenian Drama', in *Nothing to Do with Dionysos? Athenian Drama in Its Social Context*, ed. John K. Winkler and F. I. Zeitlin (Princeton, NJ: Princeton University Press, 1990), 114–15, 130–67; Florence Dupont, *Aristote ou le vampire du théâtre occidental* (Paris: Flammarion, 2007), 294–5.

Oedipus at Colonus. Oedipus becomes a blessing not for the city that expelled him, Thebes, but the one that welcomed him, Athens, which contradicts the supposed effectiveness of the scapegoat.

Once again, Sophocles's last play poses a problem. On the one hand, it shows that the sacrificial mechanism does not work for the city that put it into practice, Thebes: here, one could agree with Girard that the playwright is pointing out the futility of this primitive ritual. However, when Oedipus appears as the bearer of a blessing said to be attached to him and to accompany him wherever he goes, the ritual's effectiveness seems confirmed. It is difficult to simultaneously denounce the inanity of a sacrifice and proclaim its intact power: where would be Sophocles's consistency? This contradiction reveals one of the principal flaws of Girard's system, which requires the mechanism of the scapegoat to be ever unspeakable and inconceivable and yet sees it everywhere revealed in plain sight.

This is also the key to the ambiguous charm of this grand theory to explain the world – as with many other theories. Let us continue with it some distance further, prepared to turn back if necessary.

If tragedy's function truly is to offer the city a scapegoat, the tragic victim par excellence, what else can the perfectly innocent victim be today, following the twilight of the Olympian gods, than the Lamb of God – he who takes responsibility for man's sins, who 'takes away the sin of the world'?[81] Centuries have passed since the 'song of the he-goat' was heard in theatres: you would need to enter a church and hear the *Agnus Dei* to find its modern equivalent. Chateaubriand himself compared Greek tragedy with the performance of the mass.[82]

---

81 John I, 29.

82 François-René de Chateaubriand, *Génie du christianisme* [1802] (Paris: Flammarion, 1966), vol. 2, 69–70 (part IV, l. I, ch. VI). See also Ridgeway, *Origin of Tragedy*, 62–3; Jan Kott, *The Eating of the Gods: An*

Having completely vanished from the stage, the religious power of tragedy would then have moved wholesale to the Byzantine and Roman liturgy, and particularly in the Office of the Passion, when several voices read the narrative of the death of the Saviour and tragedy erupts around the altar. Or in the *autos sacramentales*, the plays once performed before the Blessed Sacrament to end the procession of the Feast of Corpus Christi in Spain: the similarity with the ritual of the City Dionysia is striking. Perhaps the last tragedy is not, as we believe, *Oedipus at Colonus*, but that which the church has replayed without interruption for 2,000 years, during the Easter solemnities.

Is this pure raving on the part of modern anthropology? Not quite. The first Christians were themselves aware of this proximity: in the fourth century, Gregory of Nazianzus wrote a play about the Passion of the Christ, more than half of which consisted of verse borrowed from the tragedies of Euripides:

> O beloved face, o features full of youth,
> now I cover your head in this veil;
> bloodied and bruised are your legs and arms,
> I wrap new cloth around
> your pierced and bleeding side.[83]

Does not this sound like Medea, addressing her children immediately after she murders them? Or Agave, speaking to her son Pentheus after the maenads have dismembered him? Or Joseph of Arimathea, speaking to the Lord brought down from the cross and about to be entombed? In fact, it is all of

Interpretation of Greek Tragedy, trans. Boleslaw Taborski and Edward J. Czerwinski (New York: Random House, 1973), 201.

83 Saint Grégoire de Nazianze (Saint Gregory of Nazianzus), *La Passion du Christ: Tragédie*, ed. André Tuilier (Paris: Le Cerf, 1969), v. 1469–1473. French translation based on A. Tuilier. The attribution to Gregory has been questioned (see the introduction to the play, 11–74).

the above, since Gregory is quoting and adapting verses drawn from *Medea* and *The Bacchae*,[84] in a dizzying collision of gods, heroes and religions. Is there a Pietà depicting Agave? Does Pentheus prefigure Christ? Is Christ himself, as Hölderlin suggests, 'also brother to the one saluted with Euios',[85] that is, Dionysus, the son of a mortal woman, a being dead and resurrected, and the god by whom wine is blessed? All of these figures lead by progressive analogy from the Oedipus *pharmakos* to the Redeemer of the world: *Oedipus typus Christi*.[86]

As early as the second century, the church father Clement of Alexandria seems to have been aware of a possible parallel between Dionysus and the Messiah as a danger that needed fending off. Unless the new religion took the opposite approach and exploited this proximity to solidify its foundations: fallen deities are reborn wherever they wish. This is the very argument Clement uses to convert followers of the Dionysian Mysteries and spectators of the tragic festivals to Christianity:

Here is the mountain loved by God. It is not the site of tragedies, contrary to Cithaeron, but it is devoted to the dramas

---

84 Euripides, *Medea*, v. 1071–1072; *The Bacchae*, v. 1135, and fragment III of the H. Grégoire edition of *Les Bacchantes*, 110.

85 Friedrich Hölderlin, 'L'Unique' (*Der Einzige*), first version, French trans. Gustave Roud [1967], in *Œuvres* (Paris: Gallimard, 'Bibliothèque de la Pléiade', 1995), 865. See also 'Le pain et le vin' (*Brot und Wein*), 807–14. English translations 'The Only One (First Version)', trans. Richard Sieburth, and 'Bread and Wine', trans. Michael Hamburger, in *Hyperion and Selected Poems*, ed. Eric L. Santner (New York: Continuum, The German Library, 1990), 239–43 and 178–87.

86 'Œdipe modèle (ou type) du Christ.' Gerhard Nebel, *Weltangst und Götterzorn: Eine Deutung der griechischen Tragödie* (Stuttgart: Klett, 1951), 204; cited by Jörg Dittmer, 'Die Katharsis des Oidipus: Überlegungen zur religiös-politischen Funktion von Sophokles' *Oidipus auf Kolonos*', in *Abschied von der Schuld? Zur Anthropologie und Theologie von Schuldbekenntnis, Opfer und Versöhnung*, ed. Richard Riess (Stuttgart: Kohlhammer, 1996), 47–50.

of truth, mountain where sobriety rules, in the shade of the holy forests. Bacchanalia are not celebrated here by 'the sisters of Semele the lightning-struck', by the maenads initiated into the impure sharing of the flesh, but by the daughters of God, the beautiful ewe lambs whose oracles reveal the venerable orgies in honour of the Logos and who gather in a chorus full of wisdom.[87]

The theory would be shocking had it not been advanced by one of the oldest church fathers: on 'the mountain loved by God', just as on Cithaeron, that mountain devoted to Dionysus and on which – could it be coincidence? – the new-born Oedipus was displayed, nothing is celebrated other than bacchanalia, again and forever. On the one hand, maenads; on the other, pure 'ewe lambs'; 'orgies' across the board. If this is the case, the 'drama' of Christian truth, the Eucharist, is simply a purified version of tragedy under a new name. The Ancients say so themselves. Should we take their word for it? Or should we try to be more cautious than the Ancients in dealing with such questions, despite the fact that they were far more intimate with these realities than we are today?

Similar scruples opened this chapter and will now close it, as I am led back to this Christian interpretation of *Oedipus at Colonus* so rightly criticized by Hegel and Lenormant, and which I had promised myself to treat with contempt. Here

---

87 Clément d'Alexandrie, *Protreptique*, XII, 119, 1. The following paragraphs continue this parallel. I quote from the translation by Fabienne Jourdan and refer the reader to her article, 'Dionysos dans le Protreptique de Clément d'Alexandrie: Initiations dionysiaques et mystères chrétiens', *Revue de l'histoire des religions*, no. 223 (2006): 265–82, and, more specifically, 272, note 19. See also F. Jourdan, *Orphée et les chrétiens: La réception du mythe d'Orphée dans la littérature chrétienne grecque des cinq premiers siècles, vol. I: Orphée, du repoussoir au préfigurateur du Christ: réécriture d'un mythe à des fins protreptiques chez Clément d'Alexandrie* (Paris: Belles Lettres, 2010), 416–22.

is a mystery around which countless scholars gravitate as if around a buried family secret, a mystery over which it is finally best to draw a veil. The reader was warned that the gods do not like to be spoken about. Let us keep silent: this remains the safest approach to the gods.

Our unease is not without cause. How could we have the slightest understanding of tragedy's intimate relationship with divinity if our own *literature*, far from seeking to evoke the gods, has constructed itself specifically against them and even seeks to replace them? The literary absolute debars us from the mystery of tragedy.

Epilogue

On the Unexplainable

Oedipus has no tomb. He disappeared without a trace. Vanished into thin air. With its deceptive vestiges, tragedy has not enjoyed a much more enviable fate: it is at best a mirage. As unfindable as the hero's grave.

It is time to go through the grieving process and accept our ignorance, both current and yet to come: whatever document we might still find, whatever monument we might discover (let us dream for a moment: a play by Thespis, or Sophocles's lost treatise), nothing would deliver any certainty about the origin and meaning of tragic drama – if indeed an origin or a genealogy can in and of itself teach us anything at all about a given reality.[1]

In particular, and however great the temptation, we must not search for the truth of tragedy in the tragic, or in what theatre is today – but elsewhere, sometimes very far away: in Noh, psychoanalysis, the Catholic mass. All of these practices and rituals maintain or reproduce, each in its own way, the lost powers of the arts of language.

The idea of literature is perpetually mutating, and Greek tragedy serves as an excellent point of reference to make this evolution perceptible. Relationship to place, action on the

---

1 See François Noudelmann, *Pour en finir avec la généalogie* (Paris: Léo Scheer, 2004).

body, evocation of the god: these mysteries of ancient tragedy implicitly define what our art of language is not, for it is
an art that knows not places, nor bodies, nor gods. In fact,
this is its very raison d'être: *literature*, in the modern sense
of the term, was born by severing the links that tied it to the
sensible and supersensible world. It is the delocalized and
intellectualized art par excellence, obeying a definition so
restrictive that even theatre has gradually removed itself
from literature.

Yet as contrary as it is to our habits and as foreign as it has
been to our ways of thinking, tragedy creates the illusion of
proximity. Its fortunes in artistic and literary history are
unrivalled.

Between the Renaissance and the eighteenth century, tragedy
fertilized the stage in a happy, quasi-ingenuous relationship,
inspiring theatre and giving birth to opera.

The nature of the relationship changes in the nineteenth
century with the advent of *literature*. As literature gradually
divests itself of ancient powers, a constant desire is felt to rediscover these abandoned virtues in tragedy, whether spiritual
and moral (Schelling and Hegel), existential (Nietzsche),
medical (Bernays and Freud), or political (Vernant and Vidal-
Naquet). Reasons to live are found in Sophocles, in *Oedipus*
and in *Antigone*. From Hölderlin and Kleist to Yeats and
Artaud, the tragic paradigm at the avant-garde of aesthetic
revolutions explodes the narrow framework of literature. It
is here that Wagner discovered the model for the total work
of art (*Gesamtkunstwerk*).[2] Even cinema is indebted to it:
Pasolini, Kieślowski . . . and *Star Wars*.

~

---

2 See Timothée Picard, *L'Art total: Grandeur et misère d'une utopie
(autour de Wagner)* (Rennes: Presses Universitaires de Rennes, 2006),
69–83.

A paradoxical fecundity: tragedy is a hollow shell into which everyone tries to put what they can. It has only been so productive because it has resisted every conceptual reduction – including and especially that of the *tragic*. It is impossible to have an appropriate idea of tragedy.

Kant declared that beauty is apprehended without concepts. This is the doctrine peculiar to Kantianism, which hypothesizes a 'faculty of judgement' (*Urteilskraft*) distinct from pure reason. But this position can be expressed differently and rationally: the beautiful or powerful work of art sets off a multitude of mutually incoherent ideas, none of which adjusts to the object they purport to describe. The feeling of beauty occurs when reason, faced with the profusion of possible discourses and overwhelmed by their contradictory multiplicity, gives up. A negative – or apophatic – definition of the aesthetic emotion.

Tragedy perfectly illustrates this process: it finds itself with such a powerful *aura* – to quote Benjamin – precisely because we cannot find a single reason to explain it (which makes perfect sense, given that all the keys are lost forever) while simultaneously being able to give all sorts of reasons.[3] One could also quote Gumbrecht: 'presence' is 'what meaning cannot convey'.[4]

In fact, what is true for tragedy is true for literature in general. No discourse can account for its epiphanic power or its form. We cannot talk about books we have read: we can describe the feelings they arouse, describe them and their settings (historical, cultural, social, and so on), but they

---

3 Walter Benjamin, *The Work of Art in the Age of Its Technical Reproducibility* (*Das Kunstwerk im Zeitalter seiner technischen Reproduzierbarkeit*, 1939), in *The Work of Art in the Age of Its Technical Reproducibility and Other Writings on Media*, trans. Edmund Jephcott and Harry Zohn (Cambridge, MA: Belknap Press of Harvard University, 2008), 22.

4 Hans Ulrich Gumbrecht, *Production of Presence: What Meaning Cannot Convey* (Stanford: Stanford University Press, 2004).

themselves remain inaccessible.[5] The work of the highest art is a machine to block definitive interpretation – or to multiply provisional interpretations, which amounts to the same thing.

One day T. S. Eliot received the following lines from a friend:

> Any attempt on the part of the intelligence to demonstrate the beauty of a work of art is, undoubtedly, a contradiction in terms. A rationalistic critic always makes me think of a child breaking his clockwork toy to see what there is inside.[6]

The lesson was well taken. Several years later, during a lecture at Oxford, Eliot was asked by a student what he meant by the line 'Lady, three white leopards sat under a juniper-tree.' He answered simply: 'I meant, "Lady, three white leopards sat under a juniper-tree."'[7]

This is the definition of modern art: it is self-sufficient, does not refer to any authority, and solicits every interpretation without reducing itself to any single one or to any external order – whereas ancient art, on the contrary, practised verbal transposition (*ekphrasis* was the rule) and ushered the work of art into a cosmic order in which gods

---

5 The reason we can talk about books we have not read is because we cannot talk about those we have read. See Pierre Bayard, *Comment parler des livres que l'on n'a pas lus?* (Paris: Minuit, 2007); *How to Talk about Books You Haven't Read*, trans. Jeffrey Mehlman (London: Bloomsbury, 2007).

6 Jean Verdenal, letter to T. S. Eliot, July 1911, trans. John Weightman, in *The Letters of T.S. Eliot* (London: Faber and Faber, 2009), vol. 1, 21.

7 This anecdote from 1929 is recounted by Stephen Spender in 'Remembering Eliot', *Encounter* 24, no. 4 (April 1965): 3–14; republished in *T. S. Eliot: Critical Assessments*, ed. Graham Clarke (London: Christopher Helm, 1990), vol. 1, 239. The line in question opens the second section of the poem 'Ash-Wednesday' [1930], in T. S. Eliot, *Collected Poems* (London: Faber and Faber, 1964), 87; this section had previously appeared in 1927 under the title 'Salutation'.

and mortals had their place fully prepared (as was the case with tragedy).

The next stage of the story features a kind of art known as *contemporary* (though it does not include all contemporary art), which is distinct from modern art in that it refuses the unexplainable. It tends towards pure concept. Once the works have been described, everything about them has been said: there is practically no need to see them to picture them (unlike a Chardin still life, or the *Mona Lisa*, whose quality of execution has at least as much value as the point of the project, and whose formal intensity no *ekphrasis* could exhaust). Resolving themselves in their description, these contemporary works have nothing to teach beyond their concept, other than an effect of provocation and surprise: while their presence actualizes the potential emotion contained in the initial idea, it does not modify it. It is an eminently patentable art, for its very gesture can effortlessly be reproduced all over the planet (this ease of diffusion might well be its raison d'être).

Leading the way, we find Duchamp's readymades, Christo's wrappings, and the 87 mm stripes found on all of Daniel Buren's works. In a more paradoxical way, the same is true of Christian Boltanski and Damien Hirst, though at first glance they do not seem particularly conceptual and are very different from one another. Despite an intensity of presence that is sometimes pushed to the threshold of the unbearable, their works always remain liable to a near-perfect verbalization ('a massive pile of used clothes from which a crane snatches items', 'a cow and her calf divided lengthwise and displayed in four aquariums full of formalin', and so on).[8]

---

8 Allusions, respectively, to Christian Boltanski, *Personnes*, Monumenta, Grand Palais, Paris, 2010, and to Damien Hirst, *Mother and Child Divided*, Venice Biennale, 1993.

Boltanski and Hirst are not so different from each other as they are from Anselm Kiefer, who revitalizes his art through the unexplainable, the unspeakable, the cosmos, and the gods – in short, through tragedy. In a not insignificant part of contemporary art, hermeneutics precedes the artwork, which does not exist without its justifying discourse.

With this in mind, we can define at least three ages of art and literature:

- First, the work only draws its meaning from the world: a period without art or literature as such;
- Then, the work becomes a world itself and opens itself to every interpretation: triumph of art and literature in the strict sense of the term;
- Finally, the work vanishes behind interpretation and concept: loss of mystery and the unexplainable.

Here we have the exceptional fate of tragedy, which went through all three of these phases, and is today an inlier bearing witness to an ancient world that has been almost entirely obliterated.

Now it needs to be spelled out and driven home once and for all: Sophocles did not write for us, and neither did Aeschylus and Euripides. Despite all our attempts to read a timeless message in their work (on man, the gods, fate, law, and so on), their problems were not ours.

However, *literature* does not take much notice of this: it is the great devourer, apt to swallow everything up, ingesting all the scattered texts out of context, to turn them into its own raw material. The further a work is from its source, the easier it is to integrate into the vast literary corpus.

Having lost an entire world, tragedy is the perfect victim: it fits most easily on the Procrustean bed imposed by

readings of every order (philosophical, political, psychoanalytic, structuralist, culturalist, gender, and so on). Uprooted
despite itself, it has been transformed into a literary object
by the accidents of history. The 1920s orientalist Charles
Vignier described the process as follows:

> When faced with the sight of a Scythian jewel, a Wei Dynasty
> Guan Yin, a Polynesian mask, and in general any object they
> did not have the slightest urge to admire, or even look at, five
> years earlier, high-society people have a way of exclaiming:
> 'How modern it is!'
> One forgets the object's long slumber. One endows it with
> a false permanence, when one should simply say:
> 'This object has become actual again' (today it is again in
> action).
> But we will not give in to the illusion that an object acts
> today as it did when it was made. Or think that our excite-
> ment and praise are in unison with those of long ago.[9]

Conversely, why do we not respond to Aeschylus and Sophocles like my Japanese friend who was overcome by a feeling
of terror and respect at the sight of certain ritual weapons
and sacred stones at the Musée du quai Branly? The only
artistic thing about these objects is the way we look at them
today. Surely, despite the display cases and labels intended
to domesticate them for our world, the god still lives within
them. Fear and prayer are more suited to their deep reality
than pure aesthetic emotion and formal exegesis.

9   Charles Vignier, 'Allusions à l'art chinois (fragments d'une préface)',
L'Amour de l'art, no. 1 (May 1920): 12. My thanks to Roxana Vicovanu
for introducing me to this beautiful text in her paper, 'Le difficile équilibre
du "retour à l'ordre", du "classicisme moderne" et de l'avant-garde: Le
cas de L'Esprit nouveau', at the symposium *Paradoxes de l'avant-garde
européenne: La modernité artistique entre nationalisme, internationalisme
et traditionalisme*, University of Fribourg (Switzerland), 16–18 March
2011.

In Greek tragedy, one also finds what anthropologists call the *numinous*. But to access it, one must accept the very principle of this sacred presence and power, and place oneself in an adequate psychological and intellectual state. The mystical experience will be less easy to attain than at the museum of 'first arts' on quai Branly: a ritual dagger has the advantage of existing as a material object, and the journeys that brought it to a shelf in a museum have not changed its nature, whereas the tragic texts to which we have access are only written traces of performances forever forgotten. Faced with such debris of history, with such relics of relics, alien by vocation to hermeneutic undertakings and emptied of practically any numinous presence, the temptation is great to choose silence – not the silence of contemplation and worship, alas, but that born of perplexity.

Let us praise *Oedipus Rex* to the skies, but also bury it with no qualms, along with a certain idea of Greek tragedy that is barely two centuries old. If the tomb is empty, then the void that we ourselves fill serves as a mirror: from its great distance, tragedy reveals us in our difference and gives us the ability to know ourselves. Deprived of everything that surrounded it and with which it was one, it has entered into *literature*. But it was something else before, of which we know next to nothing and that we can never hope to understand.

How, then, can I speak about this object if, on the one hand, interpretation is forbidden (as excessively *literary* and anachronistic) and, on the other, designation is impossible (lacking an adequate referent)? Caught in this epistemological bind, all I can do is to build my knowledge of the works far from the dichotomy of true and false, through a critical analysis without black and white, an approach made of grey areas of truth, of blurs and *sfumato*, of indescribable bluish horizons.

A narrow path, undoubtedly, and perhaps even an impracticable one, for today we are so deeply programmed to make meaning and truth out of everything: this is our way of inhabiting texts, for better or worse. Perhaps tomorrow things will be different. In the meantime, before we interpret, let us at least learn to suspend our intellectual machine for a moment and preserve a pure instant of grace and terror. Meaning will come next, always second compared to the recognition of our ignorance: hermeneutics with reservations.

To show the impassable limits of criticism and historical investigation is not to call for their end: on the contrary, it more easily secures their territory. As the god of Delphi put it, in everything one must avoid excess – a lesson in ethics and modesty from which knowledge is not exempt: tragedy teaches us to leave to the unexplainable its share.

Acknowledgements

My thanks to Antoine Pietrobelli, my neighbour at the tables of the Bibliothèque Nationale de France, with whom I so often discussed this book during its writing, and whose advice as an irreproachable Hellenist so often pointed me in fruitful directions; to Keeko Sakamura, who brought Noh into my life many years ago already, and whose impressions of her visit to the Musée du quai Branly revealed to me another way of thinking about tragedy; and to Gilles Philippe, *es aei*.

Thanks to Céline Surprenant for reading through Nicholas Elliott's clever translation, and to Lorna Scott Fox for her admirable copy-editing work.

Index